My Vision of Europe and Globalization

Policy Network

International.
Throughout Europe and beyond, progressive governments
confront common challenges. From school standards to modern
public services, we bring the best thinkers together to debate
the way forward.

Tackling real issues.
We put policy under scrutiny in the search for best practice and
take time to engage with the substance of debates, not spin.

Cutting edge.
Our website, publications and network of contributors give
unrivalled access to today's debates and our team keeps you up
to date with policy reforms.

For more information:

www.policy-network.net

Chair: Rt Hon Peter Mandelson MP
Founder and Director: Frédéric Michel
Deputy Director: Yasmin Holzkamm
Head of Research: Matthew Browne

Policy Network
Mezzanine Floor
Elizabeth House
39 York Road
London SE1 7NQ

T +44 (0)20 7401 5378
F +44 (0)20 7401 5371

}{ **policy network**

My Vision of Europe and Globalization

Lionel Jospin

and

The Europe We Want

Pascal Lamy and Jean Pisani-Ferry

with an introduction by
Peter Mandelson

Edited by Frédéric Michel

polity

First published in 2002 by Polity Press and Policy Network in association with Blackwell Publishers Ltd

Editorial office:
Polity Press
65 Bridge Street
Cambridge CB2 1UR, UK

Policy Network
Elizabeth House
39 York Road
Waterloo, London SE1 7NQ

Marketing and production:
Blackwell Publishers Ltd
108 Cowley Road
Oxford OX4 1JF, UK

Published in the USA by
Blackwell Publishers Inc.
350 Main Street
Malden, MA 02148, USA

Library of Congress Cataloging-in-Publication Data

Jospin, Lionel.
　[Ma vision de l'Europe et de la mondialisation. English]
　My vision of Europe and globalization / Lionel Jospin. The Europe we want / Pascal Lamy and Jean Pisani-Ferry ; foreword by Peter Mandelson ; edited by Frédéric Michel.
　　　p. cm.
My vision of Europe and globalization and The Europe we want first published in French as Ma vision de l'Europe et de la mondialisation and L'Europe de nos volontés.
　ISBN 0–7456–3029–4
　1. Globalization.　2. European Union.　3. European Union countries—Economic policy.　I. Pisani-Ferry, Jean.　II. Michel, Frédéric. III. Lamy, P. (Pascal). Europe de nos volontés.　IV. Title: Europe we want.　V. Title.
　D1060 .J59 2002
　341.242′2—dc21　　　　　　　　　　　　　　　　2002002386

Typeset in 11 on 13pt Sabon
by Graphicraft Limited, Hong Kong
Printed in Great Britain by MPG Books, Bodmin, Cornwall

This book is printed on acid-free paper.

Contents

Preface

This book is the result of a very strong working partnership between Policy Network and its authors: Lionel Jospin, Pascal Lamy and Jean Pisani-Ferry. I would like to thank them for their support since the very beginning of Policy Network. Olivier Schrameck and Aquilino Morelle were actively engaged in the project at the Prime Minister's office. Dominique Strauss-Kahn and Gilles Finchelstein started a fruitful partnership with us at the Fondation Jean-Jaurès.

My Vision of Europe and Globalization reproduces two speeches given by Lionel Jospin in Rio de Janeiro, Brazil, on 6 April 2001 and Paris, France, on 28 May. They were first published in France as *Ma vision de l'Europe et de la mondialisation* by the Fondation Jean-Jaurès (*Notes de la Fondation Jean-Jaurès*, 25, October 2001). These are followed by Lionel Jospin's address in Rennes at the last of a series of twenty-four regional forums on the future of Europe, held in France in response to the Nice meeting of the European Council of December 2000. *The Europe We Want* by Pascal Lamy and Jean Pisani-Ferry was first published in France as *L'Europe de nos volontés* by the Fondation Jean-Jaurès (*Notes de la Fondation Jean-Jaurès*, 27, January 2002). The two authors have written it in their personal capacity, with the help of a group of experts.

Andrew Adonis, as always, has been a constant and invaluable source of advice and encouragement. David Held at Polity was instrumental in developing a very challenging and timely series of publications with Policy Network, launched with *Where Now for New Labour* by Tony Giddens, and which will offer, in the coming years, a unique insight into the new ideas of progressive politics.

Yasmin Holzkamm and Matthew Browne at Policy Network managed, translated and edited this publication with great enthusiasm. Rachel Kerr at Polity made it happen.

Frédéric Michel
Founder and Director, Policy Network

My Vision of Europe and Globalization

Lionel Jospin

1

Bringing Globalization under Control

My country is fully integrated in the globalization process, in this dynamic created by the opening of markets, the movement of capital, rapid spread of technological innovations and ever-faster communications. Globalization is the reality within which we are living. But it is an ambivalent reality. It promotes global growth, yet brings growing inequality. It encourages the exploration of human diversity, yet carries within it the risk of uniformity. It releases our energies, but also brings negative forces which must be brought under control.

The course this globalization process takes will depend on the action we take in relation to it, because although globalization is a fact, it is not an end in itself. We must bring it under control if we are to enjoy its benefits and prevent its negative aspects.

Globalization therefore is a political issue that calls for a political response – by our governments.

Crucial questions cannot remain unanswered.

How can we distribute the benefits of globalization more equitably? The opening-up of economies, growth of trade, acceleration of technical progress: all this has promoted growth. But inequality is increasing between countries and within each economy. The profits of the ten largest international corporations are greater than the combined GDP of the least developed countries. Grinding poverty is the lot of nearly one human being in four.

What can we do to ensure that the accelerated growth of communications networks benefits everyone? The multiplication of information sources, increasing circulation of ideas, proliferation of new projects are all highly promising developments. But inequality in education is impeding access to this new technology. The existence of these tremendous tools for increasing knowledge can create a formidable 'digital divide'.

How can we take greater account of our planet's fragility? Our environment is not a product, a simple stock of raw materials for us to use without regard to future generations. The only real development is sustainable development.

How can we fight organized crime? It has seen a veritable explosion as a result of globalization. Ease of communications allows criminal networks to exploit differences between national laws and the weaknesses of some of them, and so escape from justice.

These are all political questions. They concern every citizen from every nation of the world. So the emergence of a global debate is a logical development.

A sort of 'world public opinion' is emerging. Association, trade union and student activists, women and men, are mobilizing all over the world taking advantage of the very dynamics of globalization: the Internet and media. In Seattle in late 1999, then in the margins of the meetings of the IMF, World Bank and Davos Forum, and more recently at Pôrto Alegre, this movement has demonstrated a growing awareness of the political issues at stake with globalization: quality of the environment, workers' social rights, consumer protection, development of the countries of the South, cultural diversity. This mobilization is welcome. But it is not enough since these forces cannot claim alone to represent the international community. The voluntary sector and non-governmental organizations have neither the accountability nor the capacity to act of the sort that are conferred by sovereignty, especially sovereignty resulting from universal suffrage. The decisive role is thus still played by states, because it's within states that political choices are prepared and made. Moreover, not all peoples have the same priorities. The developing countries are calling above all for fairer trade; the prosperous countries' concerns, crucial as they are, are not necessarily priorities shared by all.

Political globalization, therefore, remains to be built. And it has a name: regulation. Wherever there is a risk that the only effective law will be that of the jungle, where private interests damage the public interest, where the quest for short-term profit undermines social justice and harms the environment, states must define the 'ground rules'. By working together in a multilateral framework, states must build an international regulatory architecture. This requires, inter alia, supplementing and strengthening the United Nations institutions. This effort must be supported by states which, like Brazil and France, are willing to play their full part in redefining the world order.

To this end, Brazil and France are developing a common approach.

My discussions with President Cardoso have been highlighting the convergence of our views. My people – like yours – are conscious of their past, their characteristic traits and their language. They are attached to their identity, in the same way as Brazil, whose history is above all one of a meeting of cultures, intends to preserve the special legacy of this mingling of races.

This does not mean that France, any more than Brazil, is afraid to open up her country to the world. But she intends to do so in her own way, a controlled way, which takes account of her economic situation, social balance, political traditions and cultural background. Similarly, the mighty Brazilian economy is wholly dependent on international trade, and you have realized the cost of monetary turmoil linked to too-rapid globalization of the financial markets.

So, our two countries know that it is imperative to find a better way of organizing the world. How firmly they believe this is clear not only from the part they each play in the international institutions, but also from their commitment to building regional organizations. Through the European Union, France is helping to build a unified continent. For her part, with her Mercosur partners, Brazil is promoting economic development and co-operation. So we are committed to building a multipolar world, underpinned by law and the sovereignty of states.

Together, we must bring about the effective regulation the world needs.

International financial regulation

The global economy needs a stable framework.

Recent economic and financial crises have demonstrated that rules are indispensable to the proper functioning of the market economy. Over the past three years, significant progress has been made in taking on board the lessons from these crises. However, much remains to be done, particularly in the area of international financial regulation.

The reform of the Bretton Woods institutions must be pursued. The IMF now has the means to prevent the spread of a financial crisis in one part of the world. It must strengthen still further its watching brief.

Preventing financial instability also requires more transparency and more effective involvement of private players. This is why we need new prudential rules. The Financial Stability Forum has made some useful recommendations on this subject, particularly regarding the regulation of hedge funds and supervision of offshore banking. These must be fully implemented by strengthening the national laws of the states concerned and improving international co-operation. Similarly, the fight against money laundering must be one of our central concerns.

We are also working together to curtail the purely speculative volatile short-term capital movements. The goal is no different from that of the 'Tobin tax'. If it is to be a genuine measure for regulating the international financial system, then the systematic taxation of capital movements would have to be universal. I would like the International Monetary Fund to begin considering, beyond the steps already taken, under what conditions a 'viscosity' – source of stability – could be introduced into international capital movements.

Fair trade/WTO/development round

The world needs fair trade.

Half a century after the Havana Charter and the founding of GATT came the establishment of a World Trade Organization (WTO). Europe fought for the creation of this organization, which allows trade disputes to be dealt with objectively and protects us from unilateralism. This regulation is conducive to the growth of international trade.

This regulation must ensure that trade does not take precedence over all other aspects of public policy. Each nation's choices in public health, environment and public services cannot be considered solely in the light of trade rules alone. This is why the European Union wants the next round of multilateral trade negotiations, whose broad outlines will be discussed at next November's WTO ministerial conference in Qatar, to have a broad, comprehensive agenda reflecting the interests of all member countries: social progress, public health and the environment.

The world needs to share its riches more harmoniously.

Developing countries must be better integrated in the world economy. This is why France and the European Union are arguing that the next WTO conference should make this integration a clear priority. In the same spirit, France wants the new round of multilateral trade negotiations to be the 'development round'.

LDCs/ODA/debt

Without waiting for this, the European Union has decided to open its market completely to all products from the least-developed countries. It hopes that the other industrialized countries and major emerging countries will follow the same path. For all its importance, however, this decision does not exhaust our commitment to the poorest countries. These countries, which cannot yet obtain sufficient resources from trade, need official development assistance (ODA). France will go on devoting a major effort to this.

For these countries, the most important obstacle to development remains the debt burden. With a contribution of more than €8 billion, France is today the largest contributor to the initiative set in train in Lyons in 1996 to cancel the debt of the poorest countries. Forgiveness of their debts allows these countries to concentrate on their absolute priority, which is the satisfaction of the fundamental needs of their people: food, education and health.

Public health, in particular, demands the solidarity of the international community. Exacerbated by the inequality resulting from underdevelopment, new epidemics are threatening entire populations. The majority of people infected with the AIDS virus thus live in developing countries. This tragic situation demands that it be made easier for these patients to get access to the available treatment. And so I am delighted that the large pharmaceutical companies have become aware of their responsibilities and are beginning to offer differential pricing to help broaden access to affordable medicines in developing countries. All aspects of the multilateral TRIPS agreements must also be enforced; they set minimum standards for the protection of intellectual property rights, while at the same time underlining the need to limit any use of those rights which proves excessive. So those agreements must not undermine the programmes aimed at combating epidemics, but, on the contrary, be used to the full to the benefit of public health policies.

Cultural diversity

Finally, the world needs the diversity of its cultures; these must be safeguarded.

Through these regulations we are establishing new spheres of solidarity between people. This reflects what must be the ultimate purpose of globalization: interdependence among nations, the community of our respective destinies.

Peace/conflict resolution/UN/former Yugoslavia

If we know how to control it, globalization can be a new milestone in the progress of civilization. First, it can offer a new chance for peace. To safeguard peace, a stable and civilized structure of international relations must be built. Although the world is no longer divided into opposing blocs, it still is riven by complex rivalries and by ethnic and religious antagonism which fuels serious regional conflicts.

The United Nations has the prime responsibility for resolving these conflicts. Our world needs the United Nations. It is modern, because – since its origin – it has sought global solutions; its role is today perfectly attuned to our globalized world. The Security Council must remain our authority when it comes to launching collective action. In this framework, a source of international legitimacy, I believe that regional solidarity can play a growing stabilizing role. At a time when we are confronted with new tensions in the former Yugoslavia, the path of hope for all that region's people, after the re-establishment of democracy in Serbia, has to involve the prospect of ever-closer association with the European Union.

International security/disarmament

International security also requires the pursuit of disarmament. States must reaffirm their commitment to collective agreements designed to prevent the proliferation of weapons of mass destruction. In this area, France, which in the past few years has ratified several agreements – convention prohibiting chemical weapons,

Comprehensive Test Ban Treaty and convention banning anti-personnel landmines – intends to pursue international negotiations to expand the range and scope of these treaties, hoping that all this will not be seriously disrupted by the American NMD projects.

Human rights

At the same time as encouraging peace, controlled globalization can promote the blossoming of a new universalism.

This has a name: protecting human rights.

The globalization with a human face we are earnestly calling for demands proactive measures. Indeed, I do not think the spread of democratic values is an automatic and natural consequence of the opening-up of trade. Nor do I think that they can be imposed overnight by countries which, having developed them over a long period, appear today to think they have the instant recipe. Democratization is a process and, as we know, constitutes a victory for peoples.

I am convinced that we must leave no stone unturned in our quest for progress in human rights, by giving the requisite weight to these issues in our political dialogue with the countries concerned, placing conditions on aid, according priority in our co-operation to strengthening the rule of law, and even through judicious use of sanctions, provided these do not end up worsening the plight of the peoples concerned, and do not deprive us of channels of communication and positive influence within those societies.

ICC

As for the gravest violations of human dignity, genocide and crimes which are repugnant to the conscience of mankind, those responsible must be brought before an international court. The establishment of the International Criminal Court will constitute a decisive step forward in this direction.

Environment

Globalization can safeguard the future of the coming generations.

Globalization is forcing us to face up to a collective responsibility: that of protecting our environment. The one which allows us to live and in which the next generations will have to live. Since the 1992 Rio summit significant commitments have been made concerning the climate, biodiversity and desertification. The Kyoto Protocol on Climate Change and Biosecurity Protocol testify to the importance of this new awareness. But the uncertainty regarding our future climate and recurrence of natural catastrophes exhort us to implement these measures fully and prepare new initiatives.

The European Union and France are, for their part, committed to this. The position of the United States will be of key importance: I want here to signal France's great concern about the new American administration's initial statements on this issue. We must resolutely fight the temptation to abdicate all responsibility vis-à-vis future generations, solely on the grounds that unlimited deregulation of electric utilities has led to a few rare temporary shortages.

The same rationale underpins the dialogue between oil-producing and oil-consuming countries: it is essential to ensure oil price stability at a reasonable level. This stability is necessary to ensure the generalization and permanence of policies for reducing consumption of polluting energies. This is a prerequisite for stable, sustainable growth, especially for the developing countries.

Globalization is an opportunity that we must seize, a reality full of promise that we must succeed in shaping so that it benefits the whole of humanity. So we are faced with a collective choice. We can let allegedly natural economic laws guide the development of our societies, and thereby abdicate our political responsibilities. Or, on the contrary, we can seek to steer the forces at work in

Jospin : "Je suis Français. Je me sens Européen"

Le premier ministre veut renforcer l'Europe sans bouleverser son équilibre institutionnel.

France Soir : 29/5/2001

Jospin Envisions An Alternative EU

French Leader's Blueprint Sets Out a Socialist Europe

Herald Tribune : 29/5/2001

ÉDITORIAL

Continuons le débat !

Par Bruno Frappat

La Croix : 29/5/2001

economic globalization. That way we shall be able to humanize globalization and make this an era of progress for all peoples. To do this, we need countries that are fully conscious of what is at stake, responsible governments determined to take proactive measures, and legitimate and transparent multilateral institutions that respect the laws of all countries. I am convinced of this and I wanted to share my conviction with you. I believe that the international community must organize globalization in line with the law and justice. This is what our peoples expect from us.

2

On the Future of an Enlarged Europe

In fifty years, Europe has been come into being. It lives in peace, democracy prevails, our way of life appeals.

Just recently the European Union has made further progress. Growth has resumed. Unemployment is ebbing. Less than eight months from now, the euro will be a concrete reality for 300 million European citizens. A European defence is being established. The EU is reasserting its social dimension. It is acquiring the instruments needed to protect health and the environment. The French government is proud of having contributed to these changes.

Yet peoples and some policy-makers are feeling a certain disenchantment and perplexity. And it is true that the future of Europe raises legitimate questions. Does Europe not run the risk of falling apart if it enlarges to the borders of the continent? How can Europe open up to globalization without diluting its identity? To reform its institutions, should it reduce the role of nation states? How can the citizens of Europe be given a sense of ownership and involvement in Europe?

Attentive to these questions, heads of state and government meeting in Nice last year decided to undertake an in-depth review of the future of an enlarged EU. European citizens are called on to take part in it. We have decided to get this debate under way in France. My remarks this morning are a part of that process.

This is my contribution, as a policy-maker, to the discussion now beginning.

I am French. I feel European. I want a Europe which asserts its identity, is more responsive to the goals of its peoples and plays an exemplary role in the world.

This is why the debate must be about more than institutions and institutional reform. Europe is first and foremost a political undertaking, it is 'content' first and 'framework' only secondarily. Europe is made up not merely of regulations, directives and disputes. It is first and foremost a work of the mind, a societal model, a world view. The European idea as part of reality – that is what counts, as far as I am concerned. The Europe that I love, that I and countless others want to achieve, has (1) a *societal programme* (2) *a world view*, and (3) *a political architecture*.

1 Europe must proclaim a societal programme

Up until recently, the primary focus of the European endeavour was on setting up the economic and monetary union. That brought us real benefits. But now we must broaden our perspective if we want Europe to be more than just one more market in a sea of globalization. Europe is, after all, more than a market. It bears within it a societal model, the result of its history, which is taking shape in the ever closer ties being forged among European peoples. There is such a thing as a European *'art de vivre'*, a specific way of doing things, of defending freedoms, of fighting inequality and discrimination, of organizing and handling labour relations, of ensuring access to education and health care, a European pace. Each of our countries has its own traditions and rules but together these make up a common whole.

This original societal model should now be enshrined in the treaties and given practical expression in our policies. The justification for Europe is its difference. Let us remember that Europe is a civilization, which is at one and the same time a territory, a shared history, a unified economy, a human society and a variety of cultures which together form one culture.

This civilization is based on a community of values

Foremost among them are democracy and human rights The 'Founding Fathers' called for a political Europe, and then built it, in order to deliver our continent from the empire-building and murderous totalitarianism which bloodied Europe in the twentieth century. Thanks to them, Europe is now a land of peace. Yesterday's enemies have reconciled. Disunity has given way to the quest for ever greater union. Of all the regions in the world, it is in Europe that the rule of law is best implemented. Europe is the only political entity in which the death penalty no longer exists. It is the land where respect for the human person has reached its pinnacle. Europe is called upon to make this message heard more broadly.

Europe refuses to divorce economic prosperity from social progress This refusal enabled it to recover from the wars that had left it in ruins. Despite the remaining inequalities, it has today achieved a very high level of economic development. Social rights have been won – social welfare rights, trade union rights, the right to a free education.

To proclaim these values we provided the EU with a *Charter of Fundamental Rights*. The full set of principles which underpin European civilization are enshrined in the Charter – the dignity and integrity of the human person, freedoms and solidarity, equality, citizenship and justice, as well as new rights such as those which relate to the preservation of our natural heritage. This Charter deserves to be considered the keystone of the European edifice. I hope it will be an integral part of the pact uniting the nations of Europe and constituting a community of destiny among Europeans.

This community of destiny should better inspire our common policies

Europe needs more economic solidarity   The single currency has now given us a much-appreciated stability. For the last two years the euro has fulfilled its purpose as a common '*shield*' against international financial crises and competitive devaluations. To balance the structure of the EU, we now need *economic government* of the euro zone. Coordination of economic policies must be considerably enhanced. I propose that each Member State consult its counterparts and give careful consideration to their recommendations before taking decisions which have major impact on the zone as a whole. Let us set up a short-term economic action fund, to which each state would be eligible, to support any member country suffering from the effects of world economic turbulence. We must finally take action to stop any behaviour detrimental to the general European interest. Combating '*tax dumping*' is one immediate priority; it is not acceptable for certain Member States to practise unfair tax competition in order to attract international investment and offshore headquarters of European groups. Ultimately, the corporate tax system as a whole will have to be harmonized.

Economic cohesion must serve social solidarity   This is what citizens are calling for. Europe cannot be merely a free trade zone. For the last four years the French government has fought to give a new direction to the construction of Europe, focusing it more on growth and employment. Major strides were made with the adoption of the European Social Agenda. These goals must produce concrete results for all categories of workers. Working conditions must be harmonized upwards. We must reduce job insecurity and fight discrimination. Let us set the stage for a social dialogue with the trade unions at European level. A genuine body of European social law, establishing ambitious common

17

standards, must be put in place and there must be a special focus on the provision of information to employees and their involvement in the life of companies, as well as on layoffs, the struggle against job insecurity and wage policies. We must aim for a European *social treaty*.

Similarly, to guarantee equality of citizens, solidarity among them and the general interest, Europeans *need strong and efficient public services*. I am in favour of a European Directive defining the legal framework which can consolidate, under state responsibility, the role played by public services in Europe.

To promote employment, Europe must have *strong industrial goals*. Major achievements are possible with European integration – in the past, Ariane and Airbus; today, EADS in civil aircraft and, in the military sphere, the heavy transport aircraft project. These partnerships are important for our industries. They offer the resources needed for investment, lend industry the critical size needed on the world market and make it possible to avoid exclusive predominance, in crucial sectors, of the United States.

In the same spirit, Europe must assert itself as *the continent of science and innovation*. Knowledge is part of the European identity. But fragmentation of European research into insufficiently coordinated national endeavours reduces its efficiency. A true European Research Area must be set up on an urgent basis in such important fields as health and the environment, pooling its efforts as it did in space with the European Space Agency.

The unity of Europe requires stronger rights and protections for all Europeans

We must build a Common Law Area For this the Charter can serve as a reference. Under certain circumstances, it should be possible for the citizen to go directly to the European Court of Justice. We must harmonize the various national substantive and procedural rules. To start with, effective mutual recognition of court rulings and the creation of a court of arbitration to handle conflicts of national law would constitute major strides forward. I am thinking in particular of the thorny issue of divorce cases involving people of two different nationalities.

One of the fundamental rights of the citizen is security Europe must help to guarantee it.

This involves, first, *fighting crime.* Because organized crime recognizes no borders – a particularly obvious fact when it comes to money laundering, drug trafficking and all contemporary forms of trafficking in human beings – it should be fought at European level. A number of our partners have proposed the creation of an integrated European police force. I for my part support the idea. I propose the establishment of an operational criminal police force centred on Europol. Let us entrust to a specific police force the task of protecting the external borders of the EU and its international airports.

The security of Europeans also requires the establishment of a true European Judicial Area based on enhanced co-operation among judges and ongoing harmonization of criminal law in Member States, which could ultimately lead to the creation of a *European public prosecutor's office.* It would be in charge of coordinating prosecution and government legal action at European level and would in particular facilitate the execution of letters rogatory throughout the EU.

Food safety is another requirement Recent crises, particularly the *'mad cow'* crisis, have demonstrated the threat to consumers of excessively productivist policies. We must collectively learn one urgent lesson: the citizen is also a consumer who must be better protected. Let us introduce in the EU the concept of the European consumer, based on the precautionary principle, full disclosure of information and traceability of products *'from the pitchfork to the fork'.* I also propose, in the field of health care, the creation of a public health monitoring and early warning system to enable the authorities to respond immediately to a crisis when it starts.

In a world now globalized, our Europe cannot sit back as an island of relative prosperity and stability. To selfishly turn inward would be to fall victim to illusion and denial. Europe offers a model, a model open to the world and particularly to the Mediterranean and its rim. Europe is called upon to point globalization in the direction of law and justice.

2 *Europe must help chart the course for the world*

I want a strong Europe which shoulders its full responsibility in the redefinition of the world order and which acquires the means to convey its message of peace, solidarity and pluralism.

On behalf of this pluralism, Europe must foster cultural diversity

One of the most valuable parts of mankind's heritage is its diversity of cultures. And that today is under threat. The market drives uniformization of consumption patterns and concentration of cultural industries. Of course, certain forms of expression – I am thinking here especially of film – have taken on an industrial dimension. But we must protect ourselves, collectively, from the threat of uniformity and the invasion of cultural products from a single source. This is a crucial issue for civilization. This involves a struggle for European cultures, of course, but also for all other cultures: a struggle waged by Europe at the OECD, when Europe denounces the Multilateral Agreement on Investment, and within the World Trade Organization (WTO), when Europe defends the specificity of cultural creative work and cultural works. Europe must continue to act along these lines.

Conclusion du PS sur "Mondialisation, Europe, France
Intervention conclusive de Lionel Jospin

(Dimanche 31 mars 1996)

— Nous sommes en France, et peut-être pas seulement en France, devant une évolution politique significative et préoccupante.

Même si je tiens compte des obligations européennes qui s'imposent à la droite, y compris d'origine gaulliste, le fait d'être au pouvoir,

Il me semble que se sont esquissées deux reconstructions contradictoires,

— ceux qui sont historiquement de rudes proeuropéens, et c'est le cas de beaucoup de progressistes français, tendent de plus à regimber devant ce qu'ils pensent être une Europe dominée par le marché,

— à l'inverse, nombre d'eurosceptiques, en particulier à droite, peuvent se rallier à l'Europe, dès lors qu'elle est libérale

Mais en même temps, je voudrais attirer l'attention du parti sur les risques que nous pourrions courir à laisser s'accréditer la chose même que la droite que j'évoquais tout à l'heure va jouer à contre-emploi. Y compris des risques pour notre identité, dans le débat qui s'engage avec les communistes, voire avec le MDC. Le courant historique dont nous sommes les héritiers est fondamentalement européen. Rendons ce courant plus raisonnable pour nos peuples mais ne changeons pas de lit.

Europe is conscious of this issue because it harbours a great diversity of cultures   We are the heirs to these cultures in all their facets – religion, philosophy, literature, music and the visual arts – and all their expressions. They are our common heritage. For us as Europeans, culture is not, therefore, merchandise. It is first and foremost a part of our identity.

To sustain this identity, Europe *must enable everyone to share this heritage.* We must do more to foster mobility of students, artists and scientists. Ten years from now it should be possible for young Europeans to do part of their studies in an EU country different from their own. Let us make the teaching of at least two European languages from a very early age the rule. Everything must be done – especially in schools – to give our children an awareness of the fact that their national heritage is part of an even broader European heritage.

Because culture is a living thing, *it is incumbent on Europe to foster creative work.* There must be a common policy specifically designed for culture and not dominated by the rules of competition and the internal market. In this spirit I propose the establishment, at European level, of procedures to support creative film, audio-visual and information technology work and European studios. At a time when digital bouquets are being introduced in all our countries, Europe should have its own television channel patterned on the achievements of Arte.

To my mind, Europe's commitment to cultural diversity exemplifies our vision of an open international society committed to solidarity.

Taking this approach, Europe is called upon to defend peace and freedom in the world

In the face of the temptation to engage in unilateralism – that is, the might is right approach, or excessively simple viewpoints – Europe must be a factor of equilibrium in international relations.

It does not want to be a dominant power but it can use its power to serve its values.

Europe can make its voice heard thanks to a common foreign policy Let us deepen our '*common strategies*' in areas of the world where our interests are at stake. Let us strengthen the role of the High Representative for the Common European Security Policy. Let us see to it that the diplomacy of each of our nations is consistent with the definition of a policy common to us all. Let us enhance the influence, throughout the world, of an engaged and active Europe. Unified external representation of the euro zone by an elected chairman of the Eurogroup will help meet that goal. Let us introduce it as soon as possible. Additionally, the merger of the European consular networks abroad will enable '*European Centres*' to serve European expatriates all over the world. These centres will give them a heightened sense of European citizenship.

To ensure security and also contribute to peacekeeping in the world, Europe needs a common defence Its foundations have been laid. Thanks to recent decisions taken during the French Presidency of the EU, Europe is now acquiring a rapid reaction force within a permanent political and military institutional structure. The EU now needs a comprehensive doctrine on intervention and use of this force. The priority today is to strengthen a conflict prevention policy as the means of ensuring long-term security. At the same time, Europe must define its long-term defence strategy in line with its own interests and in compliance with its alliances. This means, in particular, that it must have a consistent position on the controversial missile shield initiative taken by the United States.

Beyond diplomatic and security issues, the economy and the trading system must be organized in a more equitable, more efficient manner.

23

Europe must help devise the regulation which the world needs

To prevent private sector interests from stifling the general interest, to prevent short-term profit-seeking from ignoring social justice and damaging the environment, *'rules of the game'* must be defined. The European Union can play a major role in devising regulations and act to foster three priorities.

The world economy must be given a stable framework   Recent economic and financial crises have shown that public and private sector rules are needed to make the market economy work properly. Over the last three years much has been accomplished based on lessons learned from these crises, but much also remains to be done, especially in the field of international financial regulation. Let us strengthen the role of the Bretton Woods institutions in managing and preventing crises. Let us make them more open and politically accountable. As the largest shareholder in these institutions, the European Union must make its voice heard. Let us think about how the countries of the euro zone can coordinate or even unify their representation in these institutions. Let us fight financial crime and unfair tax competition; the hesitation of the new American administration should not be a reason to call into question the work of the international financial action task force and the OECD. Europe will continue to assert its positions in favour of reforming the international financial architecture.

We want fair trade   Europe fought for the creation of the WTO because that organization handles trade disputes with objective procedures and thus protects us from unilateralism. Regulation fosters the expansion of international trade. Europe should make a case within the WTO for a trade policy which establishes clear-cut limits. Trade liberalization ought not to undermine public services, cultural diversity, social progress or food security. Europe must increase its solidarity toward developing countries to achieve a reduction in poverty. The South needs Europe. Europe will fight to help these countries take their rightful place in world trade. It will contribute to lightening the burden of debt which constitutes the main obstacle to their development.

The only development is sustainable development   The planet is under threat. We are accountable to future generations. Europe, historically an industrial heartland, a region having a high population density and poorly endowed with raw materials, has learned from the two oil shocks that the Earth is not an inexhaustible inventory of natural resources. This is perhaps why Europe is playing a leading role in the struggle for sustainable development, at a time when the United States appears to be evading its responsibilities. It is up to Europe to set an example: sustainable development is now a priority in the construction of the community. Nearly ten years after the Rio Declaration, we must go further. Europe, which spearheads the creation of a world environment authority as proposed by my government, should have an ambitious policy aimed at devising and promoting technologies which respect the environment.

Europe needs institutions worthy of its societal goals and its world view. This is where the institutional debate becomes fully relevant.

3   A political Europe requires in-depth reform

A debate is under way on the future of the Union   Conclusions are to be drawn in 2004, and we also know that they will require unanimous agreement. Therefore a consensus will have to be found among the Fifteen. We must, of course, take account of the concerns of the candidate countries. Most of them have had the benefit of democratic institutions and independence for only a decade. It is absolutely necessary that they be involved in our debate.

Jospin s'installe au centre du

Le schéma institutionnel européen de Lionel Jospin

La Tribune : 29/5/2001

débat sur l'Europe

Juncker : « J'adhère au contenu plus qu'à l'architecture »

Bonne synthèse

La Tribune : 29/5/2001

L'Europe selon Lionel Jospin

Le Figaro : 29/5/2001

Interesting contributions have already been put forward. Institutional *'models'* have been proposed. In Germany, for instance, the SPD has suggested a structure for Europe inspired in large part by the German political system. Other proposals have been and will be made. Ultimately, at the end of the process, a compromise acceptable to all will have to be sought. This is why we cannot suggest institutional structures or propose solutions without first thinking about the political meaning which we wish to give to Europe. In particular, the discussion cannot avoid focusing on the role of nations within the European entity.

I will give my view, in that spirit. I do not separate France from Europe. Like many other ardent Europeans, I want Europe but my nation remains important to me. My preferred policy would consist in building Europe without unbuilding France or any of the other European nations.

Thus I support the excellent idea of *a 'Federation of Nation States'*

'Federation' is a word which appears simple and appeals by its coherence, but which in fact has a great variety of meanings. For some the term means a European executive branch deriving its legitimacy solely from the European Parliament. That executive branch would have exclusive jurisdiction in matters of diplomacy and defence. In the new entity, today's states would have the status of the *Länder* in Germany and states in the United States. France, and indeed other European nations, could not accept that status or that interpretation of *'federation'*.

If, on the other hand, *'federation'* is taken to mean a gradual controlled process of sharing competences or transferring competences to the EU level, then the term refers to the *'federation of nation states'*, the term coined by Jacques Delors. This is a concept which I fully support. From the legal point of view it may seem ambiguous. But I believe it is politically sound, because

Europe is an original political structure, a unique precipitate of an indissoluble mixture of two different elements: the federalist ideal and the reality of European nation states.

This is why the concept of a 'federation of nation states' so aptly reflects the constituent tension which underpins the European Union There are nations, strong, vibrant nations for which identity is important, which constitute the wealth of our continent. And then there is also the determination of these nations to unite, to build an entity together, which will make each constituent part stronger. There is history on the one hand, marked by national rivalries and selfishness, and on the other hand the programme focused on harmony and alliance. Very strong federative forces exist already – the primacy of European law sanctioned by the Court of Justice, an independent Commission, the European Parliament elected by universal suffrage, the single market and the single currency. But intergovernmental co-operation still plays an important role and will remain indispensable.

If we want to move toward such a federation, we must clarify the respective competences of the EU and the states This must be done in accordance with the principle of subsidiarity. The exercise should provide an opportunity to simplify the treaties which have become indecipherable as a result of successive negotiations and the gradual accretion of common policies.

This clarification should not call shared competences into question. These foster synergies between state and EU activities. One example is training, education and culture. These areas remain within the primary competence of states; but for the benefit of all they are also subject to common policies and community programmes which should be further expanded in future.

A fortiori we should reject the re-nationalization of policies which have so far been devised and conducted at EU level. It would be odd to suggest taking further steps in the direction of stronger European integration and then start by moving backwards toward a national focus. I am thinking here in particular of structural funds. As for the common agricultural policy, it should remain at European level but be redirected. While preserving the competitiveness of our agriculture, we must help farmers to produce better to enable them to meet the demand for food quality and safety. The Common Agricultural Policy must encourage more balanced development of rural areas, preserving the diversity of our traditional rural life and agricultural practices.

But on the other hand in certain areas the *'vertical' division of competences* should be better implemented. The idea would be for the general framework of principles and objectives to be defined at European level, while political and technical implementation would be handled by either states or regions, depending on the constitutional framework and the administrative institutions of each Member State. In this way it will be possible to avoid a proliferation of detailed standards which are, often rightly – hunting is an example that comes to mind – considered excessively niggling.

A 'federation of nation states' would entail greater involvement of national parliaments in the construction of Europe Current consultation procedures between the European Parliament and national parliaments do not go far enough. Let us vest in a common body – a permanent conference of parliaments or *'Congress'* – a real political role. Meeting in regular sessions, it would monitor EU institution compliance with subsidiarity and hold an annual *'State of the Union'* debate. This *'Congress'* could play a role in amending the rules within the EU. With the exception of standards of a *'constitutional'* nature, for which current ratification procedures would remain in force, treaty changes relating to common policy technical rules could be handled, thanks to this 'Congress', in simplified procedures. This formula could replace, to good effect, the thirty or so national ratification procedures which would otherwise be needed in tomorrow's Europe. Common policies could thereby be amended far more flexibly.

As we move toward enlargement, enhanced co-operation will be indispensable   The enlargement of Europe is a historic necessity; but it is also a challenge. With the accession of new members, Europe will have to learn to manage diversity. A two-speed Europe is not an acceptable proposition. But institutional paralysis is a threat which we must ward off. Those wishing to go forward must be able to do so. This is why the enhanced co-operation mechanism was quite appropriately made more flexible in Nice. It could obviously be applied in such areas as economic coordination in conjunction with the euro, but also in areas such as health care and arms. This co-operation would enable a group of states to renew the momentum which has always driven European construction.

Our EU will also draw its strength from the vitality of its democracy.

Europe must be, for its citizens, a true political area

An area where debate is ongoing and where genuinely European political parties, like the existing Party of European Socialists, meet. An area where the peoples of Europe will be able, in electing their representatives, to make clear-cut political choices. An area where the responsibilities of those who make the decisions will be better marked out.

Europe has become a familiar horizon for our fellow citizens but they nevertheless feel a deep need for greater ownership and involvement. They want to shape Europe. For them, elections to the European Parliament should become the high point of democratic life in Europe. I call for an in-depth reform of the current election procedures. Let us find a procedure which would combine, in each member state, proportional representation and a system of large regional constituencies. This would bring the office-holder closer to the voter.

Between elections, the democratic process must not flag. In this spirit I propose three initiatives. First, direct consultation of civil society through dialogue forums. Let us build on the broad spectrum of voluntary associations in France and Europe. Let us use the new communications technologies as in the planned on-line election of the first European Student Council. Second, regular consultations held in Member States on a clearly identified important political issue which is European in nature. These consultations could take place in national parliaments or in ad hoc forums. Finally, an enhanced role for the European Mediator, whose existence is unknown to the overwhelming majority of European citizens. His role could be enhanced by appointed national or local correspondents. The mediator would then be in a position to fully fulfil his mission of resolving disputes between citizens and European institutions out of court.

The European institutions obviously need to be reformed.

The European institutions must be given greater coherence and efficiency

The European institutional system is focused on the triangle of the Commission, the Council and the European Parliament. This equilibrium remains crucial. Yet change is necessary.

The European general interest must be better safeguarded That is the role of the *European Commission*. Its political authority and legitimacy must therefore be strengthened. For this purpose I propose that the President of the Commission be appointed from the European political group which wins the European elections.

The European Parliament, as the expression of the will of the peoples, would thus be in a better position to fulfil its role as the institution to which the Commission is politically accountable and which can pass a vote of censure against the Commission. In return, the accountability of the Strasbourg Assembly should be better defined. I propose that the European Council be given a right to dissolve the Parliament on the proposal of the Commission or the Member States. This could be used in a political crisis or to resolve an institutional stand-off. An equilibrium of this kind exists, as we know, in most large representative democracies.

Like the Commission, the *Council* needs to be strengthened because it is no longer fully playing its role. The future treaty should enshrine the European Council which brings together heads of state and government and the President of the Commission. This Council should have the task of approving a true multi-year *'legislative'* programme, based on a proposal submitted by the Commission and the European Parliament. It should meet more often – for example, every two months – and concentrate, without superfluous protocol, on discussing general policy guidelines and major EU decisions.

Furthermore, the time has come to think of establishing a permanent Council of Ministers. Its members, having a status tantamount to that of Vice-Prime Ministers, would coordinate work on European issues within their own national governments. A body of this type could provide impetus, preparation and coordination of European work upstream of the European Council. In conjunction with the European Parliament, it would better fulfil its role as a co-legislator in framing European *'laws'*. In this last respect, voting should always be by qualified majority.

These are the guidelines and the reforms which I feel could underpin the institutional architecture of tomorrow's Europe.

These proposals suggest the idea, which I favour, of a European Constitution A constitution would set out the structure and the functioning of the European institutions. Of course, it would not be enough to simply call a new treaty a 'Constitution'. A text of this type would be meaningful only if it were the result of in-depth reform and not the product of a simple redrafting of the current treaties. At the same time it is important that the constitutional

33

process be a fundamental political act: the affirmation of a common goal, the expression of a collective ambition. This process would, of course, at first be conducted by governments; but it should also closely involve the citizens. The Fundamental Rights Charter would be at the heart of the Constitution. Following the method used to such good effect in the drafting of the Charter, preparation of this Constitution could be entrusted at European level to a Convention bringing together the different players in the EU: states, national parliaments, the European Parliament and civil society. Final decisions would be taken by states and ratified by peoples.

Because I am not a lukewarm European, I do not want an insipid Europe.

The Europe I would like to build is a strong Europe, conscious of its political identity, respectful of the peoples which make it up, shouldering its responsibilities in the world, prepared to support the burden of its defence, determined to preserve its balanced economic and social development model, resolved to independently define and stubbornly defend its diplomatic, industrial and commercial interests, passionately committed to its cultural diversity. The construction of Europe demands the best of all of us: ambition and imagination in vision, humility and tenacity in work.

I am determined to respond, together with others, to the call of Europe.

3

The Need for a Social Europe

The tragic events of 11 September in the United States have revealed just how vulnerable our societies are.

Accordingly, we have been led to re-examine two essential issues for democracies: the role of government, and the role of regulation and controls.

The role of government   Government action has gained added significance and legitimacy throughout the world, including in countries with the least regulated markets. It is the duty of the state to ensure the protection of the population and enforce the principles of freedom, solidarity and fairness.

Regulation   This requires the adoption of 'worldwide rules'. We must strengthen unity within Europe and improve controls.

I had an opportunity to observe, at recent European meetings on 21 September in Brussels and 19 October in Ghent, that there is a genuine awareness of the importance of these issues.

We have, of course, spoken about the fight against terrorism, including the need for co-operating at the legal, law-enforcement and financial levels, for improving the relationship between the North and the South and for dealing with critical emergencies (such as the conflict between Israelis and Palestinians).

In my opinion, however, this should not weaken Europe's strong resolve and distract us from the considerable attention being paid to the European project and the nature of European policies, by focusing on what contributes to Europe's social identity. Discussions held at regional forums on the future of Europe have demonstrated that there is considerable interest in a 'social Europe'. This was in evidence again this afternoon.

My objective for Europe is actively to promote and expand the European social model.

This social model is based on a project that does not require making a choice between productivity and social cohesion. Since the 1997 Amsterdam meeting of the European Council, we have sought to combine the economic and social objectives of the construction of Europe. And we have achieved results: the European employment strategy in Luxembourg; the full-employment objective, the priority assigned to the fight against exclusion and for equality between women and men in Lisbon. This was also the aim sought by France during her term at the helm of the European Union, when a social Europe was made one of the priorities. The European social agenda, adopted at the Nice meeting of December 2000, represents an important step in this direction.

The model also incorporates a set of principles that are now part of the European Union's Charter of Fundamental Rights, which entrenches the link between civic and political rights, economic and social rights and the rights inherent in European citizenship. You are certainly aware of the French government's commitment to ensure that the Charter will guarantee key social rights, including freedom of association, the right to strike, access to information, the obligation to consult with workers and the right to public services. The European Union's Charter of Fundamental Rights is a starting point. We must now ensure that these rights, which I want to see included in a future European constitution, are strictly implemented and further strengthened as European integration evolves in the future.

Much remains to be done. Just as there is now a European economic power, we must create a European social power for the future.

First and foremost, we must strive to make social policy serve a purpose other than just offsetting the impact of measures designed to raise productivity for its own sake. Prosperity becomes meaningful only if it brings about a reduction in inequalities, puts an end to discrimination, improves the quality of life and is conducive to self-fulfilment.

Furthermore, we must recognize that social policy can be a productive factor, and that it does not just represent an additional cost. That is why we should not become wedded to a single approach, namely the pursuit of the free-market system. That is the challenge before the annual so-called 'spring' meetings of the European Council, convened at our suggestion, which review the social and economic situation and make decisions regarding future incentives.

The need for a social Europe manifests itself today through the demand for more European control, to counter the integration of markets. At the same time, European measures must heed local differences and the specific nature of social relations, which account for such factors as the legitimate desire of citizens to maintain their national systems of social protection. Social harmonization and cultural diversity must be allowed to develop along with economic competitiveness.

In order to respond properly to these at times conflicting demands, it is important to define accurately, for each sector, what needs to be dealt with at the European level and what can be better handled at the domestic or even local level. The time has probably come to envision a new European social contract that would facilitate the choice between the interests of the community and those of individuals, make it possible to draw a line between European and national jurisdictions and clearly delineate the respective roles of labour and management. We will be making proposals on all these issues.

Social factors must always be taken into consideration when setting European Union policy. We have started to do so by defining Key Economic Policy Orientations, but other important political aspects are at issue, including the expansion of the EU, structural policy, industrial policy and commercial policy.

As far as European commercial policy is concerned, in particular, France wants next month's Ministers' Meeting of the World Trade Organization to establish a permanent working party between the International Labour Organization and the WTO, so that, gradually, social standards can be taken into account in international trade.

At the core of the European model are public-interest services, what we in France call the public services. They are an essential element of our highly valued social and geographic cohesion. Particular attention has to be given to consolidating and modernizing them.

This was a key issue during France's term at the helm of the European Union. The Nice Declaration asked for more secure financing of public-interest services and the setting up of a system for assessing their performance.

France has been circulating a memorandum among other European governments seeking to continue the process initiated in Nice. It suggests clarifying the principles and rules governing public-interest services in Europe and devising practical means to improve their performance and bolster their role.

We have had an opportunity to note during the recent emergencies that people need public services that are efficient, dependable, accessible and modern. Responding to legitimate aspirations is a key role of public administrations.

Our European social model also derives its legitimacy – and hence its strength – from an ongoing dialogue between labour and management and the participation by citizens in the European project.

The Amsterdam Treaty gave labour and management in Europe the power to affect legislation. Yet collective bargaining at the

European level remains somewhat lacklustre. Laws and regulations have been enacted at the initiative of labour and management, including those governing part-time and temporary employment. Other issues are currently under examination, such as teleworking and lifetime education, as well as specific sectors such as the textile industry. The European Trade Union Conference and the Union of Industrial and Employers' Confederations are working together to prepare the 2004 intergovernmental conference, but more momentum must be developed to achieve these goals.

Together, we must seek to identify shortcomings so as to overcome them in the interest of all. Are they of an institutional nature? Is there enough political willingness to negotiate? Has the motivation for bargaining been undermined by the recent and sometimes excessive trend to rely on coordination among Member States, at the expense of harmonization? In any event, the prospect of a new European social contract is unimaginable without a major contribution by labour and management in Europe and individual countries.

In France the government decided three years ago to establish a social dialogue committee on European and international issues. This is a place where consultations can take place between labour and management, along with exchanges with French government representatives on all economic and social topics before multilateral meetings. I believe that both labour and management are pleased with this committee. It is a valuable instrument for the decisions that we must make in Brussels, Geneva or New York.

For the benefit of our citizens, the decision-making process on Europe must be made more transparent and must no longer be restricted to limited circles of experts. In my view, the meetings held as part of this public debate on the future of Europe are only a first step, but there is much to learn from them. Let us now create a European public forum, so as to make daily, active participation by citizens in the construction of Europe a reality.

We find ourselves today on the threshold of a far-reaching reform of Europe's institutions and policies. In anticipation of the EU's expansion, we want Europe to have institutions that are more clearly defined and perceived. Europe must be governed better. For this to happen, your elected representatives must be attentive to your aspirations, and they must propose options. Nothing will be achieved, however, without the active and ongoing participation of Europeans such as yourselves.

The Europe We Want

Pascal Lamy and
Jean Pisani-Ferry

Introduction

At the end of February, 2002, the Convention on the Future of the European Union held its inaugural meeting. The Convention's mandate is large, addressing an array of subjects including the division and definition of competences in the European Union, the simplification of the EU's instruments, and the role that values such as democracy, transparency and efficiency should play in the future European Union. As with the previous Convention for the Charter of Fundamental Rights, and in opposition to Intergovernmental Conferences, the composition of the upcoming Convention is likely to be characterized by a plethora of cleavages and dividing lines. Political and national cleavages will, for example, be compounded by tensions between both executive and legislative powers, and European and national institutions.

The stakes are high. As Pascal Lamy and Jean Pisani-Ferry argue in their contribution to this debate, the future of the European Union is neither predetermined nor set in stone. The European Union of the future will become that which the political and social forces of the continent wish it to be. It is therefore important that the centre-left is clear about the challenges and opportunities this debate presents.

The current debate is a challenge, because it requires that we have a clear vision for the future of Europe. We need to be clear about what it is we wish the EU to do, the goals it should pursue. Similarly, we need to be clear about how the EU should pursue these goals, that is to say which level of governance should be attributed which competences, and which method of integration is to be used in which domains. Finally, we need to be clear about why we undertake these initiatives, so that the resulting structure is understandable to those in whose name we create it, namely the citizens. In *Pro-Europe, Pro Reform: A Progressive Vision of the EU* (Policy Network, January 2002) I have already sought to contribute to this debate by setting out my own progressive vision for Europe.

The nature of the Convention will differ profoundly from previous treaty revisions, characterized as they were by diplomatic discussions behind closed doors. The media attention that will surround it will give birth to a 'European public space', as Europe's future reform is discussed simultaneously across the continent. The debate thus provides us with an opportunity to openly discuss our visions with our partners, to convince them of the merits of our arguments. Nevertheless, we must be aware, as those on the French left have begun to realize, that Europe will not be created in our own image. We must therefore have a clear understanding of our partners' visions, their hopes, and their concerns. It is only through such an understanding that we can expect to find points of agreement that we can advocate in partnership.

It is in this context that Pascal Lamy's and Jean Pisani-Ferry's contribution, 'The Europe We Want' is a particularly welcome one. The text provides a clear vision for the future reform of the European Union drafted by two of the French left's leading figures. While the British press has concentrated on the proposals for the reform of the European Central Bank, the text itself is far broader in scope. It outlines proposals for the democratization of the EU, a policy of sustainable development, a much-needed reform of the Common Agricultural Policy, and the creation of a common judicial space, not to mention foreign policy and social affairs.

Moreover, this vision is founded on an explanation of the French left's own fears and perception of the dilemmas and challenges presented by European integration.

As always, we shall find points of agreement and disagreement with those who, in principle, share similar values and aims. However, if we are to ensure that European integration remains a project in which the dynamism of the market and social democratic values continue to thrive, if we are to build on the successes of the single market, economic and monetary union, the Lisbon Strategy, it is essential that Europe's social democrats find a means of leaving their imprint on this debate, and the reforms which it inspires. The discussions that this contribution will inspire, in Britain as across Europe, provide a healthy starting point, but one on which we must continue to build in the months that follow.

Peter Mandelson

1

The French Malaise

Having thought for too long that Europe would be built in their image, the French are now struggling to recognize Europe as it is. With the dispersion of political authority, the promotion of competition, and the questioning of public-service monopolies, they are discovering to their surprise, and often worry, that the process of European integration has gradually undermined several pillars of the model of government they thought they had exported. At the same time, the reunification of Europe, whose necessity and legitimacy remains unquestioned, is likely to reduce France's strength at the centre of the EU, with the shared future itself being played out far from its borders, in what most, if not all, still call 'Eastern Europe'. Finally, the French feel weakened in the face of a numerically more populous Germany and a more politically alert Britain.

Today this attitude is expressed through a predominantly defensive posture. Economic and Monetary Union was the last major project that the French helped bring about and helped succeed. France seems capable only of fighting to preserve its position: the paradoxical and, ultimately, powerless obsession with Franco-German parity; repeated efforts to preserve the power of the state vis-à-vis both the federalists and the regions; arcane battles to save its agricultural and cultural exceptionalism; obstinate defence of the French public services: the list could go on. The causes are often honourable, but dishearteningly defensive when they concern problems that could ultimately be addressed by Europe. Should France have no ambition but to resist the initiatives of its partners? Can it really hope that in this way it will maintain its role? When Charles Grant imagines that by 2010 France will have lost its influence through fighting too many lost battles, he assumes that these tendencies will persist into the future.[1]

As usual, this malaise is in part a complex. Formerly the purveyors of grand ideas and organizational models, the French feel ashamed that today they have no such products to export. The French state, once a model, is now, owing to its incapacity to reform, often regarded as an example of how not to do things in the view of those who are concerned about modern public-sector management.[2] Monetary debate in France finds itself caught between the German tradition, which the ECB considers itself to have inherited, and the model embodied by the Bank of England since its reform in 1997. However, no one is looking to Paris for inspiration. And it is, for example, to Spain that the Europeans turn when they wish to consider the new forms of democracy needed in a world characterized by multiple levels of government.

The French left and Europe

This malaise not only affects the left, but the left is afflicted with a particular intensity that renders inaudible its messages on regulation, solidarity, and territorial integrity. Is this because the Jacobin tradition is well represented in the left? And because, in contrast to the right, it cannot be satisfied by the sight of seeing European integration proceeding hand in hand with free-market ideology? For many free-market advocates, international economic integration is a means of dismantling national regulations.[3] The fact that our moribund Colbertism manages to wear itself out in rearguard actions against the advances of the market and competition will not displease them. But for the women and men of the left, the challenge is rather to build public rules and institutions, in Europe and *through* Europe, rules made to measure for the globalized economy. And to modernize a social system to which the left, as a political family, has already contributed a great deal. This European commitment is closely linked to the conviction that the enterprise is worth pursuing, and it is only because of this that they can accept the demolition of traditional protection. The French left has not forgotten its internationalist traditions, but getting rid of frontiers will not suffice. It also expects that European integration will remain a project to which it can subscribe, a project which will take forward the values of the left.

However, to depict the European Union as the instrument of a free-market plot would certainly be to misunderstand the enemy. Not because it remains governed, for the most part, by social democrats, but because in the eyes of the rest of the world it embodies a model of balance between the market and society, between competition and co-operation, between autonomy and solidarity. In a context of globalization and of ever-weaker forms of national public regulation, the European Union is essentially an attempt to create a public sector designed for the capitalism of today. For the states that make up the EU it is a means of influencing the rules of the game instead of simply having to adapt to them. That the EU ends up disappointing us more than it should is undeniable. But this should not hide the fact that, apart from the United States, the EU is the only actor capable of blocking the merger of two American firms, or of conducting a trade and development policy with the developing world. Neither should this eclipse the fact that despite its failings it is the least difficult place in the world to be poor. Nor should we forget that individually European Member States would find it difficult to maintain the same level of economic prosperity, of environmental protection, of consumer protection, even of social legislation. The European Union is clearly more liberal than France, but it could easily adopt Lionel Jospin's motto: 'yes to the market economy, no to the market society', and declaim it.

The French left's uncertainty is, however, justified on three points. Firstly, as with any other battle, the outcome of the political struggle over the nature of European integration is still undecided. Europe will become that which the political and social forces of the continent want it to be, and French voices carry no more than the weight and force of their conviction. The time has passed when a negotiation with just Germany was enough to make our mark on EU decisions.

It is also justified because Europe has too often been used to push through reforms that should have been considered on their own merits. France need not regret taming inflation, liberalizing trade and capital movements, ending the confusion between the shareholder state and the regulatory state, opening air travel to competition, or privatizing its banking system. But instead of being simply discussed and adopted, these reforms have been presented as necessities imposed by the logic of European integration. The cop-out has often served as short-term political comfort, and not just for the left. But what is often seen as a plot by liberal elites has most certainly undermined citizens' confidence in democracy, fed resistance to change, and has transformed the European Commission in public eyes into a relentless institution that threatens our political and social model.

Finally, this uncertainty is legitimate because the French left's European project is incomplete. After Mitterrand's second term, in the course of which plans for the continent's destiny overtook the desire to transform the country, it was natural that Lionel Jospin's political will, first and foremost, would be embodied in a goal that was as eminently national as that of employment. The fact that European affairs fall within the domain shared between the President and the Prime Minister did not make it any easier for the government to define a proactive European strategy.

Nevertheless, one must recognize that despite some notable advances – at Amsterdam and Luxembourg on employment, around the creation of the Eurogroup, at Lisbon on the objectives of social cohesion and sustainable growth, at Tampere in the area of freedom, security and justice, at Nice on the adoption of the Charter of Fundamental Rights – Europe has not been at the forefront of the French left's thinking in the past few years. Despite its traditions and the positions it has adopted – especially those of the Socialist Party – it has not succeeded in developing its analysis and defining its objectives, in a context in which the euro, the impending enlargement, and the ever-increasing preoccupations with security have all had profound impacts. Lionel Jospin's speech on Europe is thus a point of departure rather than a point of arrival.[4]

Faced with this malaise and these uncertainties, those in positions of political power might be tempted to react simply by keeping up appearances while playing a waiting game: a bit of gesticulation over symbolic challenges, flagging up the need for a constitution, here a well-chosen or well-presented nomination, there one or two flights of fancy with no consequences. But at the heart of the policy, nothing which would risk division or disquiet. We are convinced that such an approach would be doomed to failure. It would do nothing to resolve any of the strategic ambiguities that limit our choices. It would risk highlighting the dangers of the declining influence of French ideas within the EU. But it would not reassure public opinion at a time when the introduction of the euro notes and coins symbolically confirms the depth of our European commitment. Public opinion is probably less anxious about the advance of European integration than it is about the incomplete and incoherent nature of a project that everyone knows will shape our future. It is not so concerned that Europe will replace the national state in this or that field, but that the latter will depart without the former taking responsibility: that we will find ourselves in a helpless limbo where no one is responsible or accountable for successes or setbacks. Euroscepticism feeds first and foremost on the feeling that European integration is at the whim of a delicate balance between well-intentioned negotiators: negotiators armed with diverse and technocratic plans.

The European Union after 11 September

The re-examination of collective priorities and the realizations that came out of the terrorist attacks of 11 September and the start of the conflict in Afghanistan can only increase this unease. The usefulness of a European Union designed as a ship built for calm waters has been put to the test, and that test has been a hard one, since the new situation has highlighted its shortcomings. For the past fifteen years its construction has been based on several ideas: free movement within the single market, the primacy of rules with monetary union and the Stability Pact, the priority of crisis-management operations over territorial security within security and defence policy. It has been undermined on each of these three points: because, when threatened, citizens tend to prefer security to the freedom to come and go as they please, and turn towards nation states to ensure it: because the responses to 11 September underlined the United States' capacity to react quickly, reminding us of the permanence of discretionary decision-making in that country's policy, and highlighting the embarrassment of a Europe constructed on rules and procedures, whose ideal model of the world seems to be one in which there would no longer be a need to make discretionary decisions; because the new threat underlines that the external priorities which have to be dealt with are not the same as the ones Europe has chosen; and finally because in Europe the judicial affects the political and so management comes before action.

This destabilization goes further still because it underlines the fragility of the foundations on which the progress of the last fifteen years has been built. The increase in intergovernmental practices since 1992 is at the root of this difficulty in presenting a unified and dynamic response to crisis situations. Intergovernmental co-ordination only produces results if those who take part want it to, and even in the best cases they do so slowly. Insufficient concerted action, most importantly between France and Germany, in our economic responses to a common shock; the choice of national solutions to help economic sectors hurt by the terrorist attacks; the variety of strategic positions taken; the lack of visibility of a common message; and the absence of a force capable of interven-ing: all exemplify the limits of an intergovernmental system which clearly lacks method. Despite the progress made by the Europeans since 11 September in sensitive areas concerning their security – the speeding up of work on the European arrest warrant, the common definition of terrorism, civil security and closer co-operation between information services – the Member States, and particularly the three largest, have taken a higher profile than the EU in people's eyes, because they embody sovereignty, decisive-ness, security and power.

The economic question demonstrates this difficulty of action. For more than ten years, the Europeans have devoted consider-able effort towards the euro: diplomatic, with the negotiation of treaties; budgetary, with a view to convergence; economic, to adapt to the new landscape. And then, at the moment when the inter-national crisis should provide an occasion to demonstrate the benefits of an Economic and Monetary Union, we instead witness different analyses of the actors on economic policy, insufficient level of dialogue, and weaknesses of intergovernmental coordina-tion: almost as if the system which they patiently constructed had not been designed for such challenges.

It is clearly possible, indeed probable, that the new situation will result in the speeding up of integration in certain fields, as seen in the progress made on the European arrest warrant dossier. In this field and others, where the ideas were already there, the timetable will change. In the same way, the low efficacy of current military expenditure has been shown once more, which should speed up co-operation in the armaments sector. But these advances, which take place in a kind of race against events, are mostly perceived by European specialists. Citizens judge Europe by its results. And they risk discovering that in that race the EU does not make the grade.

As Paul Thibaud notes, one of the strongest critiques that has been made is that 'as far as Europe is concerned, there is a great need for clarity: clarity of action and clarity of intentions'.[5] This was the case before 11 September, and is even more so after it.

Our démarche

We clearly do not intend to offer a complete overview of the construction of Europe in this essay. Nor do we intend to propose clear-cut solutions to controversies that have been discussed at length, as if political will were enough to escape the inherent complexities of the subject matter. But we do want to help clarify the ideas of the left, and that means clearly drawing out the basic lines and making solid propositions. Some of these points of view might appear excessive; many will be seen as unrealistic. We do not formulate them in ignorance of our partners' ideas, or because we underestimate the difficulties of negotiation: on the contrary, all those who have contributed to this piece have had direct experience of such international discussions. However, we are convinced that the best way to lose a negotiation, or to lose oneself in it, is to enter it without ideas, without objectives, and without suggestions. Europe has been built on compromises made between different cultural, political, economic, and social practices and traditions. To build a compromise acceptable for all requires that all taking part know what they want and what they don't want. We want to help the French left know what it wants and what it doesn't want. And we think that there is an urgency to all of this: the French left needs to be present in the debate, launched by the European Council at Laeken, that will take place during 2002.

Since it is necessary to clarify our own ideas before making our suggestions in the final section, the second section of this text is devoted to a selective stocktaking on several key subjects in the French debate. We will give the larger part over to questions that cause reservations, worry or doubt in France, particularly to those on the left.

Notes

1   Charles Grant, *EU 2010: An Optimistic Vision of the Future*, Centre for European Reform, London, 2000.
2   On this point see the report of Jean Peyrelevade and Lucile Schmid, 'Changer l'État', *Notes de la Fondation Jean-Jaurès*, 24 (September 2001).
3   See, for example, the work of Mancur Olsen.
4   See above, pp. 3–34.
5   Paul Thibaud, 'L'Europe! L'Europe!', *Revue Internationale et Stratégique*, 42 (summer 2001).

2

Our Disenchantment with Europe

The French peculiarity

France is peculiar. On the one hand, among the founding states of
the European Community it is the one which has had the most
marked influence over its shape and structures, while, on the other,
it is one of the states that has had the most difficulty in coming to
terms with the direction that the EU is currently taking. There
are probably two main reasons for this apparent divorce: the first
is the perception of a growing influence by federal and liberal
Member States, a camp that has grown relentlessly with each
enlargement, with the result that the accent has been placed on
respecting democracy and the rule of law, and that market integration has come before the building of common policies; the second
is our own hesitation about the nature of the Europe we want.

Two points in time crystallize these tensions. The first came in
the middle of the 1980s, with the turn towards the single market,
a project orchestrated by a French socialist, Jacques Delors, who,
only having found that no other direction for relaunching European integration would have gained the support of the Member
States, set in motion the process of liberalization.

The underlying analysis borrowed from historical materialism:
at the time, businesses were the only group genuinely interested in

more integration and they were the only ones with enough weight to convince the Member States to get rid of their prerogatives. It was thus the Member States that needed pressurizing. In any case, since the Common Market, Europe has been created through economic integration. Following the setback of the European Defence Community (EDC), there was proof positive that the economic path was more powerful. We should be happy about this: in a globalized economy, Europe wouldn't exist if it had not started by giving itself an economic infrastructure.

With an imbalance thus created, Jacques Delors clearly saw the opportunity for further integration. He put in place a large-scale redistributive policy with the structural funds, and devoted much effort to fleshing out a Social Europe and bringing round trade unions to the '1992 programme'. He sought to develop common policies in fields such as the environment and research, and tried to make the leaders of Member States accept their political responsibilities. All of this meant that he was loudly reproved by the right, and particularly the British, who accused him of 'bringing in socialism by the backdoor'. But of all these developments, the first one remains the most important. The logic of the single market inexorably continues to bring its generally positive consequences, but also creates a feeling that we are building a commercial Europe that is neither political nor social.

The second decisive moment came with the negotiation of the Maastricht Treaty. Here, the logic was completely different: it was not about removing the shackles on free movement, but rather about building together a key element of economic policy, as well as a symbol of identity. This was in large part a response to the imbalance created by the Single Act. Nevertheless, the terms of the monetary compromise were hemmed in by a set of constraints that offered little room for manoeuvre: France wanted the single currency, but could only get it on German terms. While it clearly could have been done with more imagination or subtlety, monetary history was on the side of the Bundesbank at the end of the

1980s, having almost managed to make the central banks of the European Monetary System its vassals. It was on the political field that the counterweight was to be found. In effect, Germany put forward a rather confused wish for a 'political union', a somewhat vague concept based on the idea of an incipient federalism. Perhaps here was the opportunity to find a balance between monetary power and political power. But the France of François Mitterrand was not ready for that. Together with the UK, it preferred to turn the negotiations on political union in an intergovernmental direction.[1]

This double decision set the tone for the development of the European Union over the last ten years. Market integration and monetary integration have been pursued, without excluding developments in other fields, but without the latter really balancing out the former. It is in large part from this that our dissatisfactions arise, at least on the left. Dissatisfaction over the supplanting of politics, an embryonic democracy, the erosion of the public domain, the inadequacy of social policy and the procrastinations of power.

The supplanting of politics

The French regularly reproach the European Union for being too technocratic and not political enough. To them, the EU seems to be governed by a set of sectoral rules between which the will for political arbitration is missing. The central bank represents the general monetary interest of the EU, but who represents the general budgetary or structural interest? Competition policy does not support industrial policy or competitiveness. Regional policy is indifferent to the distortions in competition that it creates. Trade policy ignores its effects on employment. Monetary policy does not support growth. These examples and others give the impression that the EU is governed by a series of bureaux, each of which is, on the basis of some treaty articles, responsible for a fraction of the complete work, without there being any authority able to unify this messy ensemble, or to arbitrate between often contradictory imperatives.

Coming from a centralized country, where governing consists primarily of such arbitration, such a critique is natural. Moreover, it is largely justified: the balkanization of the EU's administration is aggravated by the complexity of the treaties, while at the same time the growth in the number of commissioners has weakened the collegiality of the Commission at a time when it should be the counterweight to the multiplication of sectoral challenges. The proliferation of specialized councils has reinforced this tendency while the declarations of the European Council, which are at once too general and too detailed, have not provided a remedy.

It is necessary, nevertheless, to be aware of the limits to this critique. The European Union is designed as a community of law that bases its regulatory authority on respecting common rules, rather than as a political community where discretionary decisions are accepted because they come from a legitimate authority. This regulation by law conforms to the political traditions in a certain number of our partner states, if less so our own. But our political culture is far from dominant in Europe and, to take just one example, the German Chancellor does not define his role in the same way as the French Prime Minister: he coordinates more often than he arbitrates.

Moreover, the evolution of international trends has often demonstrated the advantages that derive from giving certain types of decision to independent administrative authorities, working in the framework of an agreed mandate. This is the model of the central bank, a model that could in future be used for a competition authority, such as those which already exist in Member States, including France.

Finally, political arbitration, as it is practised in centralized states, gains its legitimacy from the fact that a democratic government is given the power to decide between different interests among the population. The sanction that awaits in cases of incorrect decision or biased arbitration is electoral defeat. European power is different, because while the European Parliament is directly elected, this is done on a national basis, and despite the power (as demonstrated in 1999) to oust the Commission, sovereignty does not reside in the European people. If sectoral negotiation prevails over inter-sectoral arbitration, this is because a majority decision would not necessarily be seen as legitimate. Such is the case in all federal states.

It is thus right to work towards the construction of a Europe that is more political, but we must have no illusions about what is possible, nor must we ignore the implications of the specificity of European integration.

The French economy and Europe

No one has ever risked establishing a balance sheet of European economic integration for France. Despite its great difficulty, the task is worth attempting. It clearly confirms the sense that France has done well from Europe. At the price of often painful adjustments, this agricultural country, which dealt as much with its colonies as with its neighbours and as such feared opening up to competition, has successfully achieved entry into the international economy. Today the European Union takes more than 60 per cent of our exports: it is due to trade with our European neighbours that France's position has become both qualitatively and quantitatively better than at any time in the past century. During the 1980s and 1990s intra-sectoral trade in high value-added products effectively replaced traditional inter-sector trade at the European level, and France was at the forefront of that process. At the same time, the single market has gradually become the 'base camp' from which French firms spread out beyond Europe: the volume of their direct investment in new markets shows this (€190 billion

France's trade partners in 2000: value (€ bn)

Zone	Exports	Imports	Balance
Total	327	335	−8
of which:			
EU	206 (63%)	198 (59%)	+7
Non-EU	121 (37%)	137 (41%)	−15

Source: Customs and INSEE (figures FAB-CAF)

in 2000, of which €140 billion were outside the euro zone). More recently, the euro has become a barrier against global financial turbulence.

France's recent performance in growth and job creation shows that it need not envy European countries of comparable development, even taking into account a more favourable demographic structure. One of the fruits of monetary union, gained through costly efforts, was the long-term reduction of French inflation to the level of the best performers in Europe. France has also benefited within the euro zone from a considerable competitive advantage.

Rate of growth of per capita GDP, 1950–2000 (%)

	France	Germany	UK
1950–60	1.9	3.2	1.1
1960–70	2.4	1.8	1.2
1970–80	1.4	1.2	0.8
1980–90	1.0	0.6	1.1
1990–98	1.0	0.9	1.1

Source: After A. Maddison, *L'Économie Mondiale: Une Perspective Millénaire*, OECD 2001

Inflation, 1950–2000 (%)

	1950–73	*1973–83*	*1983–93*	*1994–2000*
France	5.0	11.2	3.7	1.4
Germany	2.7	4.9	2.4	1.3
UK	4.6	13.5	5.2	1.8

Source: Index of consumer prices, 1950–83, data from Maddison (1995), available on OECD database, Economic Perspectives, December 1999, and HICP for recent figures.

France's performance appears less favourable if quality of life is considered: the most recent figures of the European Commission place the country in twelfth place in the EU in terms of GDP per capita. At the same time, these are not all that recent (they date from 1998) and, more importantly, the measures they used are not very precise: the OECD places France in ninth place, while the World Bank places it in sixth. It is more reasonable to think of France being placed with Finland, Italy, the UK and Sweden in a 'middle' group, placed between a 'lead group' mainly made up of small countries (Denmark, Belgium, Austria, the Netherlands and Ireland) and Germany on the one hand, and the Mediterranean states (Spain, Portugal and Greece) on the other.

In terms of productivity (GDP per person employed), France comes in at number four in the EU, far ahead of Germany and the UK. The median position of France for GDP per capita thus appears to be the result of very high labour productivity coupled with a below average employment rate.

The hesitations of democracy

However vexing to those who do not believe in the importance of politics, we now turn to another critique: the not-so-democratic character of European integration. This was very evident at the beginning (for the Europe of Jean Monnet did not place democratic imperatives high on the agenda) and is still valid today. Consider, for example, the Council, deliberating behind closed doors, and the number of national parliaments that find out only afterwards what their ministers have agreed to in Brussels. Of course this critique has nevertheless lost some of its bite as the Parliament's role as co-legislator has increased. At the same time, the European Parliament is only co-legislator in a little over 50 per cent of European legislation. In particular, when the Council votes by qualified majority, the Parliament is not always under co-decision.[2] Moreover, this critique keeps its full force once we move beyond the institutions and look at the concrete foundations of the functioning of democracy in Europe.

The problem basically stems from the inadequacies of the European public sphere. More than twenty years after the first direct elections to the European Parliament (in 1979), political parties remain almost exclusively nationally based (the large federations that are the PES and the EPP remain collections of national delegates and the parties that make them up prevent direct membership because they are worried about losing their own members), transnational debates are absent, and links at grassroots level are even rarer. Taken together, these political groupings have not created a common public sphere. The European debate is more often than not a collection of national debates, mostly internal to different political formations, ignoring each other even though they face similar or parallel challenges.

This is where the more meaningful deficiency is to be found, for it touches on the very basis of democracy. To cite Habermas, 'democratic citizenship is not necessarily embedded in the national identity of a people; but, whatever the diversity of forms of cultural life, it requires the socialization of all citizens into a system of a common political culture'.[3] This political culture develops through public debate on collective objectives. The state of political debate in Europe today does not allow for European-scale discussions on the political objectives which concern Europeans. This is dangerous because each new step of integration enlarges the field of collective decisions. Democracy is not possible, even with perfect institutions, if this culture does not exist and if, as a result, citizens do not decide to aggregate their votes and to accept a majority decision as legitimate, including those who are opposed to it. The experience of multinational states attests to this: without a democratic debate at the federal level, the democratic process risks turning into an intercommunity negotiation, threatened with collapse. That is why the question of democracy cannot be reduced to institutions: it is about the construction of a European society.

Civil society, which generally benefits from not having such a heavy institutional structure as political society, offers an example of a more satisfactory democratic system. Despite the weakness of social negotiation at the EU level, the trade unions have started to build a true confederation with its own internal life. Professional associations, public movements, and NGOs have also accelerated their Europeanization over the past ten years, and are able to conduct transnational debates, often under the banner of lobbying, but also in a broader sense. Transnational debate remains embryonic and limited to certain specific areas, but at least it exists: it is an example of how European democracy seems to find it easier to build from the bottom up rather than from the top down.

The erosion of the public domain

For the French the role of public services is a stumbling block in the path towards European integration for the French, and particularly for those on the left. In the name of competition, the Commission seems to be pursuing a methodical programme against the monopolies of the main public services: yesterday telecoms and air transport, today the post office and the EDF (the national electric company), tomorrow the SNCF (national rail service) or even, who knows, national education system. The fear is all the greater since this process seems to go perfectly in parallel with the processes taking place globally within the WTO negotiations. Hence, the temptation to depict the Commission as the spearhead of 'free-market globalization'.

The European response is that the French tend to confuse public service and public enterprises. Around the concept of general economic interest a doctrine has emerged that places the emphasis on guarantees of quality, of equality, and of cost offered to the user or consumer, rather than questions about the identity or public character of the entity that provides the service. The French, who invented the notion of *concession de service public*, service would be ill-advised to deny that such a distinction is not pertinent. By insisting too heavily on the defence of public-service companies, we are quickly suspected of supporting the aggressive behaviour of such-and-such a company which, being protected in its own market, can thus finance multiple acquisitions in other markets. We are thus seen as 'protectionist on the inside and predatory on the outside'.[4] In fact Électricité de France, about whom this was said, has clearly chosen to follow the path of international capitalist development.

Nevertheless, the question cannot remain at this level. It is not a question of whether the concept of a service of general interest is appropriate: it has been adopted and is clearly the only one that can cover different cultures, each of which privileges a certain type of enterprise or a certain sector. It is rather a question of knowing whether the European Union feels that it is its responsibility to promote such services across the continent. Currently, it appears that the EU is preoccupied with competition within the single market and that, under subsidiarity, the Member States have been left the responsibility of services of general economic interest.[5] This interpretation of the principle of subsidiarity is hardly defensible, since while many public services or public goods are defined or managed at the national level, others, such as railway networks and UMTS services are at least in part of an EU-wide scale, and thus call for action at that level. In the same way, there is no reason why competition for access to universal services is simply a matter for individual countries, so this should thus also be taken into consideration by the EU.

To be more concrete, the EU should not be criticized for trying to introduce competition into the rail or postal services, but it is not acceptable that it treats the issue simply as a matter of the internal market, without giving equal weight to collective priorities: for example, the environment, social and territorial cohesion, and the infrastructural requirements which follow from that. And if it is natural for the Commission to want to build an internal market in financial services, in no way does that preclude it from safeguarding conditions of access for all citizens to a minimum banking service. We don't just need guards at the temple of competition, but also architects able to invent and develop public services for the twenty-first century. This question should be on the agendas of European councils that examine the progress achieved in the realization of the Lisbon strategy, which aims to build a Europe which is both innovative and socially cohesive.

The inadequacy of social policy

The contrast between the achievements of economic Europe and the meagre *acquis* of social Europe (see pp. 74–5) is, for many French, the most tangible proof of the imbalance of European integration. How, they ask, can you build an integrated area where firms can operate without hindrance, while maintaining social legislation and negotiations almost completely at the national level? To go from that to considering Europe as asocial, or indeed fundamentally antisocial, is a step that several have made, pointing to the questioning of social norms (notably in the field of social protection by EU competition law, for example) and the effects of European integration on the power relationships between actors on the national level. European integration is seen as a factor accelerating globalization, with its cortege of restructuring, redundancies, relocations and the fatal dynamic of increased competition. Europe, for some on the French left, is primarily a motor of social disaggregation, with no corresponding counterweight of public power. And it is true that market integration has indeed called into question the statutes and particular protections which workers in certain sectors benefited from.

Others, recognizing the developments towards a social Europe, highlight the weakness and gaps relative to economic integration. At best, social policies will – after some delay – come to correct the imbalance introduced by economic integration, and some add that this state of affairs is not the result of a lack of institutional structures but rather of strategic thinking and political will. As such, the permanent gap between economic integration and space for collective action is only there to please liberals who do not want to burden the economy with social regulations.

Some clarification is needed here, however, since it relates to the objective: what exactly do we want? Should the direction of social progress be agreed at the European level? Should social norms be fixed by directives? Should redistribution operate at the EU level? Those who criticize the absence or inadequacies of social Europe are often the first to protest against intervention from Brussels, where majority decisions are made, and would doubtless be the first to denounce a retreat in social policy should a negotiation on working hours or minimum wages produce a European norm less favourable than the national one. The same people would certainly fight the unbearable liberal threat if France, in the framework of social harmonization, were to consider allowing private pensions, such as are accepted in most European countries. Attachment to national social regulations is deep, because the compromises on which they are based are often the result of long conflicts and the expression of the collective preferences of each country.[6] The symbols of social progress are not the same for the French, Germans or Swedes.

The social paradox of Europe is that if the countries which make it up undoubtedly have a common social identity which distinguishes them from the rest of the world, it is one that is embodied in different ways in each country. The difficulty in building a social Europe lies in this contradiction.

Thus the lack of balance between the economic and the social is not troubling to us, nor will we make the ritual calls for progress when we want to advance the debate. Instead, we want to clarify the foundations on which we can build together, finding the precise objectives in the search for a more realistic balance, while being clear about the concessions we are prepared to make in the name of our common project.

The procrastinations of power

The French suffer from not seeing the European Union playing the role they would like in the international arena. The alternatives suggested by Valéry Giscard d'Estaing of a 'Europe-power' or a 'Europe-space' make clear the terms of the choice. The left is no less susceptible than the right to the attractions of power, because it would like to see the continent affirm itself as a counterweight to the United States capable of influencing the definition of the rules of the international game.[7] The left would like Europe to serve as a counterpoint to what Hubert Védrine has called an American 'hyperpower'.[8] It aspires to a Europe that protects against the real and imagined pressures of globalization; to a powerful Europe able to defend its interests in the world.

This French idea is ambiguous: there are many who want to make Europe the tool of French power of yesteryear, while simultaneously refusing it the instruments of such a power. Many want it to be autonomous on the international scene, but keep Europe tied up in internal discussions. The position is certainly remarkable: there are few of our partners who share our ambition, fewer still who share our tactics.

Be that as it may, the European Union ends up moving ahead slowly. Although a power in terms of trade, able to make proposals and negotiate in this field, it has not managed in other areas to define a strategy and the means to effect it. Political co-operation, in all the various forms that it has taken over the past decades, has produced nothing substantial, even when it has had more direct interests than the United States in finding solutions, such as in the Balkans, the Middle East and the Mediterranean. Development aid, which could be a tool of policy, has not been put to the service of a specific project – even if the Europeans have tried to push their ideas on international regulation. The EU has not built up a relationship with Russia that reflects their historical and geographical proximity. It has not made the euro an instrument of international economic and financial policy, and despite some attempts has finally accepted American leadership in dealing with the crisis in Asia and with the reform of international financial architecture. In the end, it seems to know how to do only one thing: negotiate trade agreements, either bilaterally or multilaterally.

Is this self-effacement sustainable? Is it the result of latent, unexpressed disagreements between Member States and political forces on the extent of Europe's ambition? Or does it come from an institutional gap? In most cases, Europe does not say anything because it has not prepared itself to have ideas, because silence is easier than speaking, because debate is more painful than ambiguity, or because it bends to an after all generally benevolent American leadership. But also, it is often because the Member States do not want to delegate their powers in the field of external relations (the French are not the only ones to be jealous of their sovereignty). With the sole exception of trade, the other areas which have been mentioned are in large part based on intergovernmental co-operation. And if that co-operation is sometimes unavoidable, at least in the first phase, practical implementation has been the object of hesitation and variation. Too often it creates a perverse pressure to play national strategies of differentiation, without anyone genuinely taking care of the collective interests.

Notes

1   We can see this in the Schäuble–Lamers paper, where the two CDU leaders wrote of France in 1994 that 'while there is no doubt about its fundamental desire to pursue European integration, it often seems unsure when it comes to taking practical measures to that effect, with the idea always that it is impossible to renounce the sovereignty of the nation state, even though that has long been little more than an empty vessel'. In E. Colombo et al., *Réflexions sur les institutions européennes*, Économica, 1997.

2   As is the case in the Common Agricultural Policy.

3   In Jürgen Habermas, *L'intégration républicaine*, Fayard, 1998.

4   This is a mechanism through which French law recognizes the ability of private entities to provide public services, the conditions of which are defined in a contract with government. This kind of provision is widely used in the highway and water sectors.

5   Article 36 of the Charter of Fundamental Rights is illustrative in this matter. It says that 'the EU recognizes and respects access to service of general economic interest *as provided for by national legislation and practice*'. The responsibility of the EU itself is not mentioned.

6   The well-known differences between the social systems of Bismarck and Beveridge illustrate the point.

7   On this, see Pierre Moscovici, *L'Europe, une puissance dans la mondialisation*, Seuil, 2001.

8   See Hubert Védrine, 'L'hyperpuissance américaine', *Notes de la Fondation Jean-Jaurès*, 17 (2000).

3

Why Europe?

The first two sections of this essay have mainly dealt with the doubts that surround European integration and the criticisms to which it has been subjected. It is now necessary to move on to a constructive set of propositions. But before we do that it may be useful to spell out why we feel that Europe remains a project for the future and why the left should invest itself in it.

The current state of the European project

We know what drove the founding fathers and inspired their successors through to Kohl and Mitterrand: the desire to build a definitive peace between the peoples of Europe. Even today this same goal inspires those who work to reunify the continent and to establish, in the Balkans and elsewhere, the conditions for a lasting peace. For ten years now, the violent disintegration of ex-Yugoslavia has blown away our illusions, and reminded us that peace is not the product of some happy chance: it is built on co-operation and lasts through institutions. From this point of view, it is legitimate to view the weakness of the EU's initial actions in the Balkan conflicts as a betrayal of its own origins, and its current engagement as a reminder of its necessity. The engagement in Kosovo, support for the states of ex-Yugoslavia, co-operation with the Mediterranean and Eastern Europe, and enlargement itself, all demonstrate that the initial inspiration retains its strength and relevance in many of the fields in which the EU is involved. The same applies at the global level: Europe sees itself and is seen as a force for peace.

It would nevertheless be rather artificial to consider the desire for peace as the main motor of further integration between the Fifteen. To be sure, the EU's stability cannot be taken for granted, and it could legitimately be argued that reaffirming democracy, reinforcing institutions and opening new areas of co-operation is to continue working for peace. But the citizens of France, Germany or the UK, who reject out of hand the idea that one day a new war could come between them, would regard such an approach as somewhat strange.

The basic motivations for further European integration lie elsewhere. As Lionel Jospin recalled in his speech of 28 May 2001,[1] Europe also defines itself by a 'way of living' and a 'model of society' which are the products of its history. The Charter of Fundamental Rights has recently given a remarkably clear expression of this common base, even if it is clearly incomplete – it is no more than a reiteration of fundamental rights – and in some respects insufficient. The positions that the EU takes in various international negotiations – think of the death penalty, the environment, or the management of economic interdependencies – are another set of examples. As the object of constant discussion between Europeans, this common identity is often hard to see in day-to-day debates and negotiations. It becomes clear only when you take a step back.

However, such a model needs more than the preservation of a heritage to bring it to life. Economic interdependence, which remains the backbone of globalization, also brings with it the norms and values of the market economy. Competition, enforcement of property rights, freedom of enterprise, profit-driven activity: these

71

norms and values also control the economic life of our societies. But they are balanced by other norms, such as social rights, collective bargaining, equal access to public services, solidarity, and culture. Economic rules do not govern our lives without hindrance, but continually confront other laws in our society. Hence, and at the same time, we can be market economies without being market societies.

At the global level, globalization and the tensions it brings, as well as the still embryonic emergence of a planetary civic consciousness, necessitate a debate on the conditions required to rebalance the norms of market integration with those arising from other forms of interdependence. This is the heart of the discussion on global economic governance and of the debate on international trade, which places those tenets with an exclusively market-based approach against those who emphasize environmental, health and social concerns.[2] The outcome of these debates is uncertain, despite the progress made at the WTO Ministerial Conference in November 2001 at Doha on subjects such as public health and the environment. Even if a rebalancing does take place, its likely impact must not be overestimated. International trade throws together a collection of countries whose collective preferences are very heterogeneous and who thus cannot hope to agree on much more than very limited principles and procedures. We might find a mutual advantage in trading with this or that country, without necessarily sharing the same view of society or the same assessment of, or aversion to, risk. Even if rebalanced, globalization will carry with it the primacy of economic values during peaceful periods of international relations.

A more significant rebalancing might be expected to take place at the regional level (the European level in our case), because at this level collective preferences tend to be more homogeneous. This works on two levels. First, through the affirmation of objectives other than market integration, and thus the promotion of different principles and rules. Second, through a balance between competition and co-operation or, if you prefer, between negative integration, which removes barriers to the free movement of goods and economic factors, and positive integration, which develops common policies. It is primarily at the European level that we have the capacity to build the regulations to frame and balance the development of markets.

In this respect, the European Union is an unparalleled organization. It has invented a method for mediating between the national and the global levels and it has designed a model of open regionalism. From the southern cone of Latin America to East Asia, it is regarded as the laboratory for new types of relations between people and states. This might sound like an idealistic dream, as the dissatisfaction already mentioned tends to suggest. However, frustration with the present should not hide the progress made. Most notably, the Europe under construction is not doomed to be dominated simply by the needs of the market. Integration in this field is more or less complete and almost all the various paths that further integration is taking lead to different objectives: building a common economic policy, co-operation in home affairs, social development, etc. To put it differently: a Europe where the dynamic of integration was blocked would certainly be destined to become a mere economic area; a Europe which advances is by its very nature a richer proposition.

To these motivations a final argument must be added which, while well-known, does not become any less relevant: an EU which knows what it wants is able to alter the shape of the world while the individual Member States no longer can. This is true of globalization: in fields such as trade, environment, finance, development and others besides the EU is, or could be, a player. This is true in peacekeeping, security, the fight against fraud, and anti-terrorism. Of course, on particular occasions a given state might be able to show its singularity, work as a key player, block a negotiation, or play the honest broker. But such episodes are illusory, and do not last long.

Force for peace, model of society, laboratory for international relations, global player: the French left can recognize itself in each of these European identities and should endeavour to ensure that in each of these areas its voice is heard. The debate at this level is more demanding than at the national level, since much of that which is normally taken for granted has to be explained and argued, as those who have taken part in European discussions will know. The fact that the compromises which result from such discussions are often unsatisfactory is testament to this. But that should not hide either the importance of these challenges or the open character of the debate on the choices for the future. The conclusions of the Laeken European Council of December 2001, and the choice of a broad mandate for the Convention on the Future of Europe, reflect this openness.

To fulfil the roles expected of it, the European Union must, however, advance. Sadly, it currently seems to be exhausted.

Rebuild the dynamic of integration

A double breakdown

For the last fifty years, European integration has alternated between leaps forward and periods of consolidation. While it looked unsure after the stalemate of the European Defence Community, the quarrels of the 1960s over supranationality, the economic setbacks of the 1970s and the recession in the early 1990s, the EU has turned each of these moments of doubt into new advances. This dynamic rested on two pillars, one institutional the other political: the Monnet method and the Franco-German alliance, both of which seem to have broken down.

The Monnet method, rather than seeking to set end goals for the EU, sought to put in place powerful integration mechanisms, the best example of which is the *acquis communautaire*, whereby the transfer of a competence to the EU level is irreversible and is to be accepted by all future members. Through this system states have more than once agreed to transfers of sovereignty which they would have doubtless refused if they had been asked to accept them initially. However, this approach is contested today, precisely because it overlooks the question of the end-goal of European integration and because it allows the transfer of competences in only one direction. The introduction of the principle of subsidiarity in the Maastricht Treaty, with its philosophy of decentralization, marked a first limitation. The declaration annexed to the Nice Treaty, which establishes the objective of 'establishing, and maintaining thereafter, a more precise delimitation of the competences between the European Union and the Member States', is a further step. Introduced at the request of Germany, where the *Länder* were demanding guarantees against the encroachments of Brussels, the notion of delimiting competences is effectively the exact opposite of the Monnet method. If it is adopted with a rigid interpretation it could ossify the division of roles between the EU and the Member States, instead of ensuring a degree of economic integration and a desire to build together.

The Franco-German couple has been the political motor of Europe for many decades, less for strict reasons of power than because the two countries bring together the essentials of Europe's diversity, and so appear as the only 'core' acceptable to all the Member States (as opposed to meetings between the French, Germans and British: the legitimacy of such meetings is always challenged). But for some years now, this relationship has failed to fulfil its function, and in turn has contributed to depriving the whole of Europe of a vision for the future. The breaking of parity between the two countries at Nice will further complicate its functioning. At the same time Tony Blair has put forward a project and expressed a desire to lead, but its credibility is subject to caution given indecision on the strategy to follow (a directoire of three with France and Germany, or a search for alternative alliances) and, moreover, due to the deep uncertainty of the British public as to its relationship with Europe.

This double breakdown comes at a time when the European Union faces several key challenges: the introduction of the euro, which can only increase the expectations, and indeed the needs, of citizens vis-à-vis the European institutions; enlargement, which by its size and the diversity of countries involved will be more a change of nature than a change of scale; and the creation of a common defence and security policy, which makes sense only if put to the service of a shared model of European strategic interests.

Three challenges: the euro . . .

It is easy to underestimate the impact of the euro, since nothing spectacular has happened since 1 January 1999 and the continent's politicians have shown a singular lack of enthusiasm. However, an essential stage has been reached with the introduction of notes and coins. It is a qualitative leap forward, in three ways:

- through the symbolic and political meaning imparted by the pooling of monetary sovereignty;
- through the depth of the engagement. Europeans have put their well-being in the hands of the monetary institution that they built. History reminds us of the horrors that a poorly managed currency can cause;
- through the nature of this integration. Integration is no longer simply a matter of fixing the rules of the game, as it was with the single market, but also about taking decisions of macroeconomic policy that will directly affect economic agents. With the euro, Europe has created for the first time an institution whose decisions are awaited because they will directly affect inflation, economic activity and employment. Thus European integration has taken a decisive step towards real policy-making.[3]

There is, however, a debate about the federalizing impact of the euro, because Europe continues to hesitate between two views of monetary integration, which Maastricht tried to reconcile. On the one hand, there are those who, in the fashion of the gold standard of the nineteenth century, seek to depoliticize the currency, ensure that it is managed as much as possible by a set of fixed rules, placing the onus on societies to make the adjustments required for monetary stability. On the other hand, there are those who, in the tradition of the twentieth century, regard monetary policy as one of the instruments of an active macroeconomic policy, which takes responsibility for reacting to shocks and attempts to minimize the adjustments imposed on society. These two views are both compatible with the goal of price stability and a scrupulous respect for the central bank's independence. Rarely expressed explicitly, this key choice underlies all of the debates about the single currency.

This is why the euro does not *a priori* have an integrating impact. It will only have one if the federalist view of the currency prevails – if those who support that view propose it, fight for it, and enter into alliances. If they do not, then there is a great risk of disillusionment and the tensions could be acute.

. . . Enlargement . . .

Enlargement of the European Union has been on the agenda for over twelve years, when the countries of the former Soviet bloc began their long return to Europe. The date, shape and means of this European reunification have long been shrouded in uncertainty, to the point that one might doubt it ever happening. But the situation has become ever clearer and the current course of negotiations leads one to assume that there will be twenty-five members in 2004, if the Commission's big bang scenario is achieved, or twenty-seven, if enlargement includes all the countries with whom negotiations have started.[4]

The extension of the EU to the countries with whom negotiations have been started[5] will increase its population by a quarter and the number of members by three-quarters. It will also increase its diversity considerably. Economic and social diversity, measured by the ratio of income per capita between the richest and the poorest countries, which was only 1:1.5 in 1950s, and 1:2.5 following Greek and Irish membership, will probably rise to 1:5. After enlargement, 36 per cent of the population will live in regions with per capita GDP of less than three-quarters of the EU average. In the long term, enlargement will certainly create efficiency gains for the whole of Europe, just as the transition has already created very substantial gains for the candidate countries themselves. However, it remains true, in the words of one notable Hungarian economist,[6] that while the Europe of today is integration through the market, post-enlargement Europe will be integration by development. This is a major redistributive challenge for the EU.

Saying that and simply underlining the difficulty of the enterprise is not enough. The enlargement now under way will also increase the political and cultural diversity of the EU since it will include countries who only recently regained their political sovereignty and who will doubtless be much more jealous of their national prerogatives than the current members. For that reason, the candidate countries are motivated less by the idea of shared sovereignty than they are by the desire to assure their security, and to resume their history by removing the barriers of Cold War Europe.

While it is true to say that the necessity of enlargement is written into the history of the continent, that enlargement will bring the European enterprise back to its initial goal of reconciliation and peace, and that, more prosaically, it offers Western Europe the chance to reinforce its capacity for growth by increasing its economic integration with less developed countries, the challenges it poses should not be hidden. Beyond the budgetary tensions and the need to reform the structural funds and the CAP, the challenge is at once institutional, economic and political:

- *Institutional*, because the Nice compromise has not produced a legitimate or efficient system. Between a system of weighted votes which promises to paralyse decision-making,[7] a Commission too numerous for the responsibilities it has,[8] a bank whose board will be numerically weakened vis-à-vis the governors of the national central banks,[9] and an overcrowded Parliament,[10] the entire system will be overburdened and weakened.
- *Economic*, because above and beyond the well-known problems caused by the reform of the CAP and the structural funds, the Europe of the past twenty years, the Europe of the single market and monetary union, has been based on the presumption that participating states were all similar. Enlargement to very diverse states, whose administrative systems are also very unequal, constitutes a strong test.
- *Political*, because the motivations of the candidate countries are not the same as those of the architects of the European Union, and because a Europe this numerous and diverse will be able to move forward only with a high degree of political will.

This diagnosis has been around for several years. Logically, it should have led to these problems being addressed prior to enlargement, given that it would be paradoxical for the countries of Central and Eastern Europe to prove themselves more audacious than the current members of the EU, when they are still in the phase of rebuilding their national identity. That path was not taken. That means simultaneously dealing with the question of enlargement and deepening, since a European Union of twenty-five members which relies on the Nice Treaty runs the risk of a dilution that would be hard to reverse, and which in turn would call into question the dynamic of European integration.

In the light of an enlargement which will be both large and quick, the countries which carry the European project need to find answers to the questions of ends and means that are being asked today. Without a new political impulse to the dynamic of integration, what can one expect from a Europe of Twenty-five exhausted before it was even born?

. . . Defence

European defence has made much important progress of late. With the Franco-British initiative of St Malo (December 1998), followed shortly after by the Fifteen, the EU can now use a range of political, military and diplomatic resources. It is putting in place a rapid reaction force of 60,000 soldiers, ready to be deployed from 2003 for crisis-management missions.

The implications of this initiative should not be misunderstood. We are not building a European army; it is not about ensuring territorial defence, a question which remains exclusively with the Atlantic alliance; the budgetary resources earmarked for defence in Europe remain limited, and costs are high owing to the delay in integrating defence industries. Nevertheless, the beginnings hold out great promise, since if it is to meet its goals the EU will have to go beyond the quantitatively modest efforts of Helsinki, move to integrate defence manufacturing (and particularly armaments) and formulate a common strategic doctrine.

The operations in Afghanistan and the more general strategic reorientations caused by the attacks of 11 September have underlined the distance between the ambitions and realities of today. The EU hid behind the Member States, and more particularly behind those which had both a strategic culture and the capacity to project military power. It is still too early to say whether this new environment will result in an acceleration of European security and defence integration, or instead make the lack of common will all too evident. It is, however, certain that the future of the

EU will be played out in no small measure on this subject. It would not be overstating the case to say that in the next ten years questions of security and defence will become as important an issue for European integration as monetary affairs have been during the last twenty. One effect of the priority of defence will be to put the British in the centre of things. The UK will be an essential actor in these areas, especially since it currently has the best capabilities for external projection.

Which direction?

The simultaneity of these three challenges is the cause of much confusion for Europeans. For more than eight years, reflections on a new integrative force have abounded. They have most often sought to balance the weight of numbers by some form or other of differentiated integration. From the 'core' of Wolfgang Schäuble and Karl Lamers[11] to the 'vanguard' of Jacques Delors,[12] to the 'centre of gravity' of Joschka Fischer,[13] and the 'pioneer group' of Jacques Chirac, they have all dealt with the same idea. Some, like Dominique Strauss-Kahn, envisage forming this vanguard around the euro.[14] Others put their hopes in a relaunch and institutionalization of Franco-German co-operation.[15] Others still, like Hubert Védrine and Pierre Moscovici, imagine the impulse will be given by those countries which take part simultaneously in all the areas of reinforced co-operation.[16]

The logic of this démarche is that the counterpart to the coming enlargement is to be found in decisive progress towards more integration between those countries which want to move ahead. The coexistence of different formulas, however, illustrates the difficulty of the task. To different extents, they all pose the same problems:

- The first comes from the extraordinary force of attraction of any grouping hoping to reinforce integration. As was seen in the stalemate of the 'Confederation', the episode of the European Economic Area in the 1980s,[17] and, generally speaking, the euro, centripetal forces are systematically dominant because each country worries about having to submit to the law of a centre of which it is not part. To some extent, the logic of European integration is the opposite of that of Groucho Marx, who used to say he didn't want to be a member of any club that would accept him: in Europe, everyone wants to be a member of those clubs which might otherwise shut them out.[18] The fear of negative effects for blackballed candidates strengthens that tendency.

- The second arises from the institutional difficulties which underlie any arrangement based on variable geometry. If it is a simple political grouping, it is quickly suspected of trying to become a directoire; if it is organized co-operation, there are immediate difficulties caused by the overlapping of institutions and procedures. In either case, the question of the democratic legitimacy quickly arises.

- The third problem relates to the future of reinforced co-operation. This option has been available since the Treaty of Amsterdam, and will be made more accessible if the Nice Treaty is ratified, but to date the option has not been used and one might well wonder whether it will be used in the future in any significant manner. Some think that the provisions will, in the end, not allow fiscal co-operation among several Member States, as might once have been expected, but will instead permit only the grouping of countries around a sea or along a river.

- Finally, and concretely, there is the British question: a centre of gravity which excludes the UK could not pretend to speak for Europe in the fields of defence, foreign affairs or even financial matters. But were the pound to join the euro, the size of the centre would risk becoming so large that its meaning would be in doubt.

The difficulties which stem from a vanguard project are thus important (and lead certain observers to feel the idea is stillborn and that the best thing to do is reflect on the conditions in which one could organize a rearguard). It should be added that despite the appeals made by Schäuble and Lamers and Joschka Fischer, it is far from clear that the idea attracts wide support in Germany. The risk is thus that the project remains a fantasy which distracts us from the reality of the current situation.

From this analysis, we draw the conclusion that the French left should retain the option of inviting those who want to step up the speed of integration to build a European core: the timeframe for this project could be much quicker than we realize today. But we also conclude that this perspective should in no way stop us from focusing on the current paths of development. Our immediate future will be in the Europe of Twenty-five and we cannot be absent from the debates that are going to take place about it.

Notes

1 See above, pp. 3–34.
2 See Jean-Louis Bianco and Jean-Michel Sévérino, 'Un autre monde est possible', *Notes de la Fondation Jean-Jaurès*, 20 (March 2001) [part I]; 23 (July–August 2001) [part II].
3 This is certainly not the first time that discretionary responsibilities have been given to the EU. In particular, the decisions of the Commission in merger control fall into this category. However, the impact of monetary decisions is of a much greater dimension, as citizens will appreciate.
4 The big bang is seen today as a way of not leaving Poland outside. However, the scenario poses another important question, namely the fate of Bulgaria and Romania, a question which has been posed by France.
5 That would exclude Turkey, which is officially a candidate but with whom negotiations have not begun.
6 Andras Inotai.

7 See Frédéric Bobay, 'La réforme du Conseil de l'Union européenne à partir de la théorie des jeux', *Revue Française d'Économie*, 14/2 (October 2001), and Richard Baldwin et al., *Nice Try: Should the Treaty of Nice be Ratified?*, Centre for Economic Policy Research, Monitoring European Integration Series, 2001.

8 The Commission will have, at least in the first instance, one member per state.

9 If the structures of the ESCB are not reformed, the Council of Governors will have one member per state taking part in the euro, and the number of members of the board will remain six.

10 The European Parliament will have 732 members after enlargement.

11 Wolfgang Schäuble and Karl Lamers, 'Réflexions sur la politique européenne', in E. Colombo et al., *Réflexions sur les institutions européennes*, Économica, 1997.

12 Jacques Delors, 'Pour une avant-garde européenne', *Le Nouvel Observateur*, 25–31 January 2001.

13 Joschka Fischer, 'De la confederation à la féderation', in *Quo vadis Europa?*, *Notes de la Fondation Jean-Jaurès*, 16 (July 2000).

14 Dominique Strauss-Kahn, 'Reconstruire l'Europe à partir de l'euro', in *Quo vadis Europa?*, ibid.

15 See Jean-Noël Jeanneney, Pascal Lamy, Henri Nallet and Dominique Strauss-Kahn, 'Europe: pour aller plus loin', *Le Monde*, 19 June 2001.

16 See Pierre Moscovici, *L'Europe: une puissance dans la mondialisation*, Seuil, 2001, as well as the report of Jean-Louis Qermonne's group for the Plan, *L'Union européenne en quête d'institutions légitimes et efficacies*, CGP 1999, which advances for the first time the idea of a centre of gravity created by the intersection of areas of reinforced co-operation.

17 The European Community proposed a new organization based on a single market to the members of the European Free Trade Area (EFTA). Most of the countries involved in these negotiations finally ended up as members of the EU.

18 The idea of Schäuble and Lamers was based on the hypothesis that monetary union would cover only a minority of Member States.

4

Eight Paths to the Future

The eight paths examined in this section cover a broad range of fields. As well as the main issues of the day, we address some issues which have not received a great deal of attention up to now but seem to us to be important, either because the left has accorded a particular value to them, or because they impinge on the way the left frames the debate. Although long, such a list is still necessarily selective. It leaves aside areas that deserve to be developed, such as education, research, and regional development, among others.

Find the means to make enlargement
a success

Since Nice, the alternative of 'widening or deepening', which had long dominated debates, has been overtaken. Each term now has its own timetable, and neither can be considered to come before the other. Whether we are happy or sad about this, the priority is how to make the two compatible with each other, so that once it is prepared and put into perspective, enlargement can be used as an opportunity to relaunch European integration.

Pascal Lamy and Jean Pisani-Ferry

Get to grips with the challenges

If the EU is to cope with the challenge of enlargement it cannot be by simply imposing the formal respect for the 'Copenhagen criteria' (a democratic system, the mechanics of a market economy, and the ability to take on the *acquis communautaire*). It must help reduce all the structural barriers that, as a result of their difficult history, stand in the way of convergence: administrative shortcomings, gaps in the law and judicial systems, the absence of decentralized structures capable of supporting the action of the structural funds, and the embryonic character of civil society, to name but four. The EU should thus help build a base upon which a genuine economic and social integration of the new members can take place. In so doing, however, it will be confronted by problems that previous enlargements did not prepare it for, such as the control of external frontiers, or the treatment of minorities.

The shock will be as much cultural as economic. By the end of the negotiations, the candidate countries will have experienced ten years of adjustment guided by the objective of membership. Their fatigue is already clear; it is expressed through more reserved attitudes towards accession. It can be predicted that once they enter into the EU, a number of the new Member States will be very reluctant to consider any new qualitative leap forward in the integration process.

Moreover, the very notion of integration differs strongly between East and West. The Fifteen look on enlargement as a means of improving the conditions of economic and social development across the whole of the enlarged EU, as well as offering the continent extra guarantees of peace and stability. For the candidate countries, the desire to join the EU is based on their willingness to demonstrate their belonging, mark the irreversibility of political and economic reforms, integrate economically, and benefit from the support of the EU. This commitment does not automatically translate into a desire to deepen the process of European integration.

Membership is a moral and historic right in their eyes, the payment of a debt. It is thus invested with a spiritual dimension, one coupled with a right to solidarity. Combined with the fatigue, this attitude could weaken a method of construction that has as one of its pillars the creation of a community of law. If ignored, it could become the source of potentially destructive misunderstandings in the future.

The mechanisms of integration are, themselves, the issue here. EU law has – up until now – been considered as primarily ensuring the functioning of a single area in a common timeframe. However, the increased gap in levels of development engendered by enlargement raises questions about the flexibility of EU law when faced with a new dilemma: either we integrate this diversity and difference into our legal framework, or we drift into legislative gridlock in sectors where the single market has not been completed. This same is true for the skilful decision-making mechanisms based on compromise and co-operation that have been established and experienced. Each Member State has learnt, sometimes at its own expense, that in the long term there is more to be gained through compromise than confrontation or the use of force. In contrast, the candidate countries' reconstruction occurred through their peaceful but unified opposition to Soviet power. Their recently acquired independence (in 2004, when accession takes place only fifteen years will have passed since the fall of the Berlin Wall) is a focal point for their identity, one which often translates into a deep attachment to their sovereignty. The theme of subsidiarity, for which read attacks on the 'Brussels bureaucracy', will be more than ever the order of the day.

Move on from the conservative vision of Agenda 2000

Confronted by this reality, the silence is deafening. Anxiety and questions abound, but no political approach has been put forward that really emphasizes the significance and the basic challenges of enlargement. Discussions concentrate on the consequences for the candidate countries, for the institutions, or for common policies (the budget, CAP, structural funds, etc.), as if a collective schizophrenia has led us to cut the difficulties up into small pieces so that we might better avoid the truth of the entire situation.

This collective inability to think about or set out the consequences of enlargement for both the structures and the project arose at the Lisbon European Council of 1992, when the principle of enlargement to the East was first accepted, but regarded as a distant event. As such, the necessary parallel reforms which should accompany enlargement were not put in place. Both Jacques Delors, President of the Commission (then at the height of its influence), and François Mitterrand tried to raise the issue at the time. But the European Council did not want to listen. Since Lisbon, and increasingly so as the deadline draws nearer, prior reforms have been regarded as a factor that could potentially block negotiations, and thus have been forbidden. However, any substantial reform attempted after enlargement will be made all the more difficult because it will be seen by the new members as an attempt to change a contract that has already been much negotiated. This is the Lisbon paradox: no reform can be done beforehand, but neither is anything possible afterwards.

Faced with the novelty of the question and its political urgency, the EU has reassured itself by turning the problem into a collection of sectoral negotiations, just like the negotiations it is used to. This is even more paradoxical as, since 1973, most enlargements have been as much a negotiation among the Member States themselves, in order to adapt the *acquis*, as it has been between the EU and the newcomers. The entry of the United Kingdom, for example, raised the question of national contributions to the EU budget, which they attempted to resolve through the creation of regional policy; similarly the accession of Spain and Portugal would not have been possible without a major increase in efforts to improve social and economic cohesion. When such negotiations did not take place – as with both the Greek enlargement and the last enlargement – then the difficulties of this approach became, *a posteriori*, all too apparent.[1]

The deeper reason for this collective myopia is, as is often the case, to be found on our own doorstep, namely in the incomplete nature of European integration itself. If the Member States have set off without a route map for the enlargement process, it is because they have not come to terms with their own relationship with the EU. Prioritizing the common interest would have implied setting conditions that individual diplomatic interests sought to avoid.

After Nice, the maintenance of unanimity in fields vital to the success of enlargement – the structural funds, tax and social policy, and, *de facto*, financial perspectives – now limits the ability of the EU to react. Finding a consensus between old and new Member States on a package is deeply compromised, because the new Member States will upset the balance between the net contributors and the net beneficiaries of the EU budget. The main losers will make any agreement impossible if they are not compensated, even though the EU's efforts have already helped their own economic recovery. Indeed, the success of their efforts to catch up has led to calls to end this support. Without an overall political vision that allows each Member State to find a balance in the financial reform, unanimity writes off the decision-making process post-2006. Between now and then, inability to reform the CAP and structural funds – which together constitute some 80 per cent of the EU budget – risks draining the accession negotiations of much of their content.

The limited redistribution and stabilization mechanisms of the EU make this situation even more dangerous. Redistribution mechanisms are likely to be in great demand, given the degree of catching-up that is required of the new Member States. It would be reassuring to believe that simply relying on the forces of competition within the single market, corrected at the edges by structural funds and regional policies, could ensure this 'catch-up'. But one must ask what the European response would be if that proves not to be the case. The implicit contract to which the new members prepare themselves to sign up is that, in return for the considerable adaption efforts they are expected to provide when they join the EU, they will find a framework favourable to their catching up. Should the economic environment take a turn for the worse, one might expect that budgetary solidarity would be in much greater demand. The simple growth in the number of members increases the risk that sectoral shocks will seriously affect the growth of a country whose economic base is not sufficiently diversified. Similarly, even if the East and West of Europe are already well integrated, the losses and gains caused by enlargement will be unequally distributed, and certain regions or countries will suffer more than others. In an Economic and Monetary Union framed by budgetary discipline, there is no guarantee that such a shock could be absorbed without reinforcing the current stabilization mechanisms.

Finally, despite numerous attempts and demands, little progress has been made in organizing the relationship between the different levels of government in Europe, or to move towards making the Member States and their institutions more accountable within the framework of the competences defined in the Treaty. Devolution, decentralization, regionalization, the transfer of certain activities, etc., all remain largely unexplored. The EU thus risks becoming permanently torn between taking on unsuitable missions, and the temptation to renationalize entire sections of common policies to the detriment of the single market and the equality of the Member States. For the new members, who gambled a large part of their democratization efforts and development initiatives on the difficult process of establishing decentralized structures, such hesitation could appear particularly counter-productive.

This inertia translates into the absence of a budgetary framework capable of responding to the challenges of enlargement.

On the expenditure side, the Agenda 2000 expenditure limit of 1.19 per cent of GDP will not be sufficient to ensure an equitable treatment of the new Member States in comparison to the current status as 'accession candidates'. Nor, for that matter, will it be sufficient to match their efforts in investment and restructuring. The ceiling for structural aids (structural funds and the cohesion fund) of 4 per cent of national GDP, agreed at the Berlin European Council as being 'reasonable', effectively translates into a level of per capita aid clearly lower than that which currently prevails in the cohesion countries. Maintaining this ceiling will be politically untenable before, but especially after, enlargement.

Moreover, the need to assist the candidate countries in 'taking on the *acquis*' – notably in the fields of health, environment, transport and energy – is not included in the current budgetary structure, nor is there any mention of the push necessary to put in place administrative structures and efficient legal systems.

As far as receipts are concerned, the ceiling on appropriations of 1.27 per cent of GDP, the multitude of sources of finance, and the corrective mechanisms (limiting the VAT base to 55 per cent of GDP, the British rebate) combine to make the system of EU resources impenetrable and inequitable. This system, which dates from the 1992 Edinburgh European Council, could reduce the EU to a classic international organization where members greedily haggle over their contributions. This complexity and the lack of democratic control also place the very legitimacy of the EU budget in greater danger. If expenditure were to increase to meet the requirements of enlargement, this legitimacy would be further weakened since the debate on certain Member States' net contributions would once again come to the fore.

Put differently, enlargement poses difficult questions about the EU's resources with a new acuteness. Initially based on a proper EU resource, customs duties, the EU's finances have turned into a system of national contributions that are neither very transparent nor legitimate, and which have opened the door to all the haggling.

It is now time to recast it and to finance the EU budget with a specifically EU-based direct tax system.

Finally, public opinion has not been properly prepared for the impact of enlargement. Within the EU, people are certainly favourable to the principle of reunifying Europe,[2] but they see enlargement as a long-term perspective, and are worried about its effects on employment and security. In the candidate countries, the demand for a right to membership dominates, while the capacity for change has found its limits. Everywhere the idea is growing that the major project of enlargement has been undertaken with a complete lack of democratic transparency and no collective control over means and ends.

Anxieties and fears can lead to the search for scapegoats: 'Brussels' and its attacks on local customs, immigration, liberalization, etc. As recent elections have shown, the resurgence of populism and extremism is not limited to either West or Central and Eastern Europe. Faced with these risks, neither the discourse nor the political reality has produced a clear perspective for citizens. The EU's political leaders have made commitments to the candidate countries, but have neither tried to explain to their own electorates why enlargement is necessary, nor where and how they themselves will need to adapt. More meaningfully, a positive attitude towards an enlargement, often described as a reconciliation, presupposes that there is an awareness of other Member States. Within the EU, such an awareness was achieved through cultural, tourist and family exchanges, which developed over the course of decades. Cultural exchanges between the East and West of Europe are minimal in comparison. There are practically no projects that facilitate this meeting of peoples, either because there is no EU competence (education and culture, for example), or because there is a lack of financial resources (as is the case for research and universities). Such initiatives should be prioritized in order to combat the lack of knowledge that breeds fear and feeds populist politics. It is also necessary to allow direct co-operation between regional groups in the East and the West to develop. Such co-operation is an irreplaceable step in the emergence of a civil society, without which economic and social development would run the risk of becoming like a 'Potemkin village'.

Take the opportunity offered by Laeken

The opening of a wide debate on the future of the EU agreed at Nice, with a timetable that matches that of enlargement, offers an historic opportunity to break through the current impasse and to reconcile – finally – widening and deepening. The formula of the Convention chosen at Laeken as the means to prepare for the 2004 deadline offers us the opportunity, if we know how to take it. All the more so because the Convention must not only identify solutions to the challenges of enlargement, but more importantly, must also contribute to a redrafting of the European pact. It must address the question 'why live together?' in Europe.

The Convention allows for the immediate involvement of the candidate countries in the elaboration of the project around which the institutional face of an enlarged Europe might be redefined. Indeed, it has a new and original blend: of state representatives and the Commission, or European and national parliamentarians, combined with an openness towards civil societies. The Convention is a one-off chance to develop an active learning process, allowing us to face up to the cultural dimension of the impact of enlargement. It is, in fact, a process in which all participants will be involved, not as critics of decisions in which they have no part, but as players in a team, building a common future. This procedure also offers the possibility of developing a democratic debate on the means and ends of enlargement, for both the citizens of the fifteen Member States and the candidate countries, a debate which was previously non-existent. The fact that this debate will be encouraged to take place under the scrutiny of different public opinions cannot but give it – as the French experience with decentralized forums testifies – a human dimension of contact with others, and one that can spontaneously create an openness of spirit and understanding.

However, it is not about having debate for debate's sake. To escape the contradictions that surround enlargement, it is vital to base the European project on a new contract: between the old and new Member States on the one hand; and between the EU and its citizens, on the other. The first element of this contract would deal with issues of institutional reform, the urgency of which is only reinforced by enlargement. The second element should be a convergence pact between the EU and the candidate countries, so as to support their economic catch-up. The objective would be structural convergence, with the means coming first of all from a redeployment of Structural Funds in favour of the new members. This would be completed by an investment programme of the Cohesion Fund,[3] co-financed by the EIB and if necessary, in a groundbreaking innovation, by Member States who wished to take part.

Such a programme should cover transport, energy, telecommunications, research and development, and the environment, and could give rise to structural trans-European projects, but also to administrative, health and basic public service structures (education, health, police, justice). For this, a reform of the EU budget is essential. Reform of the CAP, detailed later on, should provide the opportunity to clarify its structure, end the special treatment of the British contribution, explicitly end the claims of the net contributors to the EU budget, and gain the agreement of the 'accession candidates' on the redeployment of the Structural Funds. More fundamentally, the evolution of EU expenditure should allow for a reorientation towards the most innovative sectors. As regards receipts, the removal of the 1.27 per cent of GDP ceiling is required in order to finance this new expenditure, and the creation of a European tax would be both a simplifying and legitimizing factor. As regards expenditure, without calling into question the multiannual programming of financial perspectives, the introduction of genuine sources of flexibility will be essential if the EU is to be capable of reacting to asymmetric shocks.

Thereafter it is necessary to develop exchanges within the wider Europe, by investing in European education and media, and by strongly favouring direct co-operation between regional and local governments from East and West. Lastly, it is necessary that the public debate on the future of Europe should feed into an information programme on enlargement on the same scale as that used for the switch to the euro. A special programme, going far beyond the current basic information campaign, should be put in place in all the countries, both members and non-members, before the conclusion of enlargement negotiations.

We propose:

- *Putting in place the means necessary for the debate on the future of Europe, in which the candidate countries are participating, to become the opportunity for meaningful exchanges that are diffused – as much as possible – through the public.*
- *A convergence pact between the EU and the candidate countries, based on (a) a redeployment of the Structural Funds in favour of the candidate countries, and (b) a programme of investment designed to help the catching-up and integration of the new members.*
- *A reform of the EU budget which would cover the CAP and Structural Funds, accompanied by a reorientation of expenditure towards more innovative priorities such as research and development, and raising the ceiling on resources in order to finance enlargement. It will be necessary to start discussions before 2006 on reform of the CAP and Structural Funds.*
- *A programme of cultural and educational exchanges, grants for student exchanges, as well as the encouragement of decentralized co-operation between regional groups.*

Reinvigorate European democracy

Democracy is a basic element of the European idea. The EU has all its necessary attributes and yet Europe still suffers from a lack of democracy. The second part of this essay has stressed the shortcomings of the European public sphere, the absence of a transnational civil society, and the lack of a common political culture. This dimension is essential, because democracy does not exist simply by virtue of institutions. Its exercise presupposes a sense of belonging – historically, taxation and the creation of a redistributive function has been the decisive expression of this; a genuine debate among citizens; and forms of organization that go beyond the national. That is why we have formulated some proposals below that seek to encourage the creation of a common public sphere for the peoples of Europe. However, the institutional dimension of the question cannot be avoided, especially since the European Council decided, in the Laeken Declaration, to open a very large debate on the institutions.[4] We start with the role of the European Parliament and national parliaments, and move on to the conditions for governance of the EU.

Involve civil society usefully

Democracy is based on participation. For that, encounters of different views between civil society in all its forms (citizens, businesses, NGOs) and the representatives of political institutions is essential. That is why public opinion, citizens and civil society actors should become fully involved in the functioning of the EU and take part in its reform. That should take place through the publication of debates (of the Council, Commission and Parliament) on the choice of objectives, and through regular consultations on the policies that have been implemented. The Convention offers a chance to launch this movement by including participants from civil society as observers and through the associated consultation procedures. We cannot let this opportunity pass. It is a chance, in the words of Philippe Herzog, to create the conditions for a 'plurinational participatory democracy'.[5]

The European Parliament, an institution lacking legitimacy

Beyond the establishment of a European civil society, the deepening of democracy takes place through a reinforcement of the institutions, and in particular the Parliament, the only representative of the European people. However, disappointment with the EP prevails. Like all parliaments, it is a forum where different currents of thought confront each other. Like all others, it exercises a power of nomination and of control, a legislative power and a budgetary power. However, it enjoys neither the profile nor the legitimacy of its national counterparts. Europeans do not identify it as the institution where the political debate takes place. It is the object of much criticism, often very harsh, and appears – all at once – to lack legitimacy, proximity, legibility and transparency. The body that is supposed to contribute to redressing the 'democratic deficit' of European integration sometimes thus gives the impression of aggravating it through the establishment of a new enlightened bureaucracy, concerned above all with the extension of its own powers.

The origin of this problem undoubtedly lies in the fact that the European Parliament was created under the illusion that it was sufficient to transpose the recipe and the ingredients for a national parliament onto the European level. For some time it seemed that for this transposition to be successful all that was needed was a steady increase in the competences and powers of the institution. That has been done. And yet, the Parliament still fails to give the impression that it has reached maturity or achieved a position of influence. That said, there cannot be a political Europe without an assembly where European political debates can take place.

The first power of the European Parliament, enshrined in the treaties, is that of control. It exercises it over a number of European institutions and bodies. The attempt by the Socialist group in July 1994 to veto the choice of Jacques Santer as head of the Commission, and then the resignation of the same Commission under the threat of a motion of censure in March 1999, illustrate the reality of this power. But the Commission is now fragile, and its relationship with the European Parliament has not regained the degree of trust necessary for the EU to function properly. As for the Parliament, judging from the low turnout in the European elections that followed, it did not gain any legitimacy from using its power of control.

In terms of legislative responsibilities, MEPs enjoy more powers than many MPs. However, this power is limited in three ways:

- Firstly, the real competences of the European Parliament are to be found in the 'first pillar' of the European Union, namely the EU pillar. In the *Common Foreign and Security Policy* pillar, it is merely kept informed and can adopt non-binding resolutions; in the *Justice and Home Affairs* pillar, the Parliament's powers lie somewhere in between.
- A second limitation arises from the sharing of legislative competences with the Council. While, for example, the French distinguish between laws and regulations, there is no hierarchy of norms at the European level, which inter alia results in a blurring of the division of executive tasks between the Commission and the Member States. As a result, the Parliament is stubborn with regard to anything that could reduce its legislative power.[6]
- Third, co-decision is not systematic: in many areas, including agriculture, which represents a key part of the EU budget, the Parliament's power is limited. The result is that some policies, though essential, are not put under any effective parliamentary control, either at the national or EU level. This is the case in the common trade policy, where the competence was transferred to the EU, but not under co-decision.

The low turnout at the last European elections has led to questions about the legitimacy of an institution that interests less than one elector in two. Overall, the European Parliament is ignored by public opinion, which does not consider it responsible for the evolution of Europe. It embodies the stalemate that characterizes European democracy more generally, and it is unable to impose itself in peoples' minds as a centre of power.

This feeling is particularly noticeable every five years during European elections, which voters use as an opportunity to vent their feelings about national politics. In effect, citizens vote in a kind of national letting-off of steam, which does not correspond to the way votes are translated into seats in the assembly itself. They do it all the more freely because MEPs, in France as in many other Member States with national lists, suffer from a lack of proximity to their voters, and because the voting system favours a proliferation of lists.

In these conditions, the European Parliament does not play the role of the transnational representative of the European 'people'. It is more like an assembly where national delegations retain importance to the detriment of political lines of division. Thus, it generally triggers unanimous opposition. But still Europe needs a strong parliament, the manifestation of a popular will, the symbol of a public sphere. If we want citizens to support the pursuit of European integration, then it is necessary that they understand how its democracy functions.

How can we move forward?

The first answer is to be found upstream of institutional debates: it consists in creating the conditions for the emergence of a European political culture. While the inadequacies of European public culture have been addressed earlier, several reasons to suppose that a public sphere could develop in Europe were also identified. It is necessary to promote this idea, firstly by removing the obstacles to a transnational civic life, and then by encouraging forms of European expression.[7] In the political field, we should encourage the decompartmentalization of national political debates, and develop genuine European political parties by favouring the elections of MEPs on a transnational basis.

The sceptics will doubtless object that if this political dimension does not exist, it is because there is no demand for it from citizens. However, the debate about globalization, the humanitarian movement, and militant environmentalism testify to the fact that citizens are deeply concerned by transnational issues. There is no reason to think that they could not express themselves in European debates – given that it is these discussions that will have effects on economic, political and social choices in the future, rather than just focusing on impenetrable quarrels.

The second response lies in a change to the voting system for European elections: it is essential, in France at least, to bring in regional lists, in such a way that citizens can clearly identify their representative.

The third response deals with the priorities of parliamentary work. The European Parliament should debate important subjects, subjects which matter to citizens, and should concentrate its legislative activity in the fields in which it is undisputed. This could be done by introducing a hierarchy of norms, between laws and decrees, as in France, or by adopting a call-back procedure, as in Britain.[8] It is also necessary to change its form: the deliberative and formal style of the speeches in an empty assembly is impossible to see in a positive light from the perspective of the European citizen. What is needed is a parliament that is full of energy, argumentative and even oppositional: a parliament where the debate runs along transnational political lines of division, and where questioning and spontaneity are not forbidden, but managed. The current reform of the Parliament's rules of procedure could contribute to this, if it does not get lost in the meandering procedures to which it is accustomed.

The fourth response resides in giving the European Parliament tax powers. The fact that it has responsibilities only over expenditure is a factor that both reduces its accountability and weakens its democratic credentials. It also contributes to its bias in favour of spending.

However, to reach maturity, the European Parliament must take a major step forward, become a genuine chamber of the people and politicize its work. However inconvenient, the recent election of the Parliament's new President without a preliminary accord between the PES and the EPP is a step in the right direction. It is clearly necessary to go further and renounce the *a priori* practice of dividing up positions of power between the political groups. In the same way, choosing the Commission President on the basis of the results of the European elections could give the latter a higher profile, reinforce the authority of the person chosen, and increase the politicization of the assembly.

What type of government?

To limit the question of democracy simply to a discussion of the role of the European Parliament would be excessively reductionist. The inadequacies of democracy in the EU are profoundly linked to those of the system of government, or, if you prefer, governance, as underlined during the last ten years by the rejection of the referendum on the Maastricht Treaty by the Danes in 1992, the size of the French No vote in the referendum of the same year, and the Irish No vote in the referendum on the Nice Treaty in 2001.

The shortcomings of European governance are well known. They spring from the tangled responsibilities that prevent citizens from distinguishing between the powers of the EU and the Member States, the Commission and the Council, or the Council and the Parliament:

- The executive and legislative functions are closely interwoven with one another, since the former is divided between the Commission and the Council and the latter between the Council

101

and the Parliament, and since the specificity of the Council's legislative role is presented in published debates.
- The political system of the EU suffers from an illegibility that stems from the coexistence of two types of governance: one, in the first 'pillar', the 'EU' model; and the other intergovernmental, in the second and (to a lesser extent) third 'pillars'. Moreover, the movement of the EU pillar towards intergovernmental practices, with the development of coordination procedures, has further complicated the structure;
- the legal order of the treaties is obscured by the absence of a distinction between acts of a constitutional nature and acts dealing with ordinary legislation (in France, the latter are decrees).

In sum, the citizens of the EU cannot hold the institutions or those who belong to them responsible for the decisions that affect them. Neither can they ask them to explain how they have exercised the responsibilities that they have been given. Transparency and democratic responsibility are thus handicapped by the complexity of the legal and institutional edifice. In the end, the legitimacy of the institutions, and of European integration itself, is thus weakened.

It must be noted that the deficiencies that are problems today, in a Europe of Fifteen, will be intolerable tomorrow in a Europe of Twenty-five. Several facts show that Europe's leaders have accepted that the shape of tomorrow's EU cannot simply be left to diplomatic negotiations. Consider the debate on the future of Europe launched after the Nice European Council, for example, and the opening of discussions on the division of competences that will set the scene for the preparation of the next treaty revision. A Convention, bringing together government and Commission representatives, as well as European and national parliamentary representatives, has been put in place. The establishment of a forum to engage more closely with civil society on these constitutional discussions has also been announced.

To establish legitimate and democratic institutions, the federalist option offers a route that is strangely criticized in France. Yet, it is not intrinsically more centralizing than the current form of governance in the EU. Its objective is to create a system of government at several levels by articulating the responsibilities of those different levels and ensuring the democratic function of the whole.[9] In any case, the EU already has institutions (the Court of Justice or the ECB, for example) and policies (in trade and in competition) that are clearly of a federal nature. The federal inspiration could thus be a source of progress for European integration. It does not have to be refused *a priori*, as if it implied agreement to drop any claim to national autonomy. The opacity of the current system and the absence of clear principles probably do a far greater disservice to the nation and democracy than a well-framed federalism would. A number of proposals flow from this – ensuring awareness of Council deliberations when it sits as a legislature, ending the designation of members of federal institutions (Commission, Council or ECB) on the basis of nationality, making the Commission accountable to the Parliament – that would all increase the legitimacy and legibility of the EU's institutions.

The question is to know just how far this approach is capable of responding to the current problems. There is a double difficulty in this. On one hand, the reality of the European Union is that Member States take part in the executive function in some fields, whereas in a purely federal organization their function would be principally legislative. This is increasingly the case, as and when integration covers new areas. In certain cases, it is a matter of learning to co-operate, before delegating executive responsibility to a common body. In others, the situation is unlikely to change, because the instruments necessarily imply co-operation between states instead of delegation to a federal body. This has happened in the economic field, with regard to budgetary policy: the essentials of public expenditure and tax remain the responsibility of the Member States, when a classic federal solution would have implied the transfer of an important part of income and expenditure to the federal level. The situation is similar in the field of defence: the states want to co-operate on common actions, but are not ready to transfer their means. More generally, the advance of European integration in constitutional areas implies more and more co-operation between states.

The concept of a Federation of Nation States is a response to this overlap of responsibilities. It is not a catch-all term that falsely tries to reconcile two opposites. Rather, it clearly states that the basic units of the federation are the states and that European integration, if it is to be effectively organized around an executive pole (the Commission) and a legislative pole (the Parliament), must also specify the involvement of the Council in these two. If it is not to become sterile, the complexity of this construction requires that the Council play its part efficiently. The growing number of EU competences, the continual and increasing overlap of national and European action, and the elevation of the Common Foreign and Security Policy (CFSP) and police, justice and immigration co-operation to the ranks of common policies suggest that the coordination functions of 'general affairs' and the function of foreign affairs need to be distinguished. This implies the creation of a General Affairs Council made up of ministers who are readily available and who are linked to arbitrations within each government.

This clarification should extend to the European Council. Turning it into the permanent supreme body for orientation and leadership requires:

- That it effectively concentrates on essential issues, that is to say that its meetings are prepared by the executive coupling of the Commission and the new General Affairs Council, and that its decisions are implemented by the legislative coupling of the Parliament and Council. Organizing the work of these three institutions under an easy-to-understand agenda, such as Tony Blair has suggested, would be a useful improvement on current practices, provided the Commission's right of initiative is preserved.

- That the incursions of the European Council into legislative and executive matters will only happen in exceptional circumstances, in order that it maintains its role as a supreme body. Nevertheless, when it does, respect for the rule of law means that the European Council, when it acts as a legislative body, must abide by the common rules of the Council (same majority rules, respect for the rules of procedure, co-decision with the Parliament if it concerns a legislative act).
- That the democratic legitimacy of the Commission should be reinforced, confronted as it is by a directly elected Parliament and a European Council made up of the highest elected offices in Europe. A minimal re-balancing could include implementing the 'Delors proposal' (which would forge a link between the choice of the Commission President and the European Parliament elections). Another means of reinforcing the Commission's legitimacy would be to make it accountable to the European Council.

We propose:

- *Implementing provisions conducive to the development of a European public debate: procedures for direct membership of European parties, in particular the Party of European Socialists; adoption of a statute of non-profit European associations and foundations; the definition of a framework for associations 'in the general European interest' for those foundations or associations that are active in at least two countries of the EU and that have a general European interest, allowing those who make donations to get the same tax exemptions as are already available in Member States for public-interest associations and other foundations; the definition of a legal statute for European professional organization.*

- *European Parliament elections in France to be held on a regional list system, as is already the case in many of our neighbouring countries.*
- *Making the Council debates public when it sits as a legislative body.*
- *The introduction of a dose of transnationalism into the European Parliament. This could be done through the direct election of some MEPs on a European-level proportional representation system, as the Laeken Declaration suggests, or by a more incentive-based system, which is our preferred option. For example, it might involve a specific public subsidy of €1 per vote received for all transnational lists gaining at least 5 per cent of the votes in the European Parliament elections. A list would be considered as transnational if in each country at least one-third of the listed participants were non-nationals, and it ran for election in at least half the Member States, covering at least half the electorate.*
- *The clarification of the priorities of the European Parliament. For the Parliament to concentrate on political rather than technical matters, it is necessary either to adopt a hierarchy of norms, or to design a well-framed Parliamentary call-back procedure.*
- *During European Parliament elections, the main political groups should propose their choice for the presidency of the Commission. The President would then be designated on that basis, according to the previously noted suggestion of Jacques Delors.*
- *Making the Commission accountable to the European Council, which would be able to dismiss it.*
- *Reform of the General Affairs Council, so that coordination tasks are given to ministers who are readily available and who are linked to the work of arbitration within each government, and the establishment of decision-making procedures for the European Council when it sits as the 'Council of Ministers meeting at the level of heads of state and government'.*

- *A distinction between constitutional treaty provisions (the 'basic treaty', according to the Laeken Declaration), and those which come from ordinary legislation. Enlargement necessitates the adoption of treaty revision procedures that do not need the unanimous agreement of all Member States, which implies a differentiation between the two types of provisions, so that non-constitutional amendments can be made more easily.*

Building a common economic policy

In France the left have not had the monopoly of support for the euro, but (without counting the decisive choice to stay in the European Monetary System in 1983) they have supported it at two key moments: during the negotiation of the Treaty on Economic and Monetary Union, and at the point of transition to the single currency. However, some on the left still remain uncertain. Is it necessary to develop a common economic policy, or is it simply enough to manage the currency while being indifferent to developments in the wider economy? This hesitation runs through all the debates about the euro.

What is the euro for?

On balance the three first years of the euro have been positive, and not just with respect to the series of catastrophes predicted by its critics. In 1998–9, faced with the Asian crisis, and then again in 2001, with the slowdown of the American economy, the single currency effectively prevented international shocks from disturbing the European economy, as has been the case in the past. The European Central Bank[10] has been responsive to internal and external shocks, although sometimes with some delay, and generally without succeeding in clearly explaining the reasons for its choices. It demonstrated greater pragmatism than was generally expected of it, and certainly helped the European economy better to resist the shocks, which it would not have been able to do under the old monetary regime.

However, the future is less certain. Despite three years of learning how to live together, the monetary, budgetary and exchange rate policy doctrine have not yet stabilized. The position of the ECB in the EU system of governance remains unsatisfactory. The coordination of economic policies, which lies with the Council, has been accepted in principle, but not really in practice (except if it is considered limited to the Stability Pact). In sum, the economic policy system of the euro zone, which is by its very nature more complex than other fields of EU decision-making, remains the subject of heated discussion. Debates on principles, conflicts of power, and uncertainties about the means of collective leadership all handicap the operational capacity of the European institutions, even though the troubled international environment requires a decision-making capacity that is fast and assured.

Enlargement will, necessarily, amplify these difficulties. The new Member States will not all be able to join the euro quickly and, based on the Swedish experience, some might not even wish to join. For the convergence criteria that decide on a country's ability to join the single currency to be all defined solely in nominal terms was conceptually weak but empirically acceptable, given the general proximity of the different economies and the long history of monetary rapprochement. But it would be hazardous to apply them, tomorrow, to the new candidates without first asking questions about the structural rationale for the adoption of a single currency, and without assessing the risk of instability that economies and societies in the process of catching up and of integration are exposed to. The idea that the euro is part of the *acquis communautaire* and thus has to be imposed on the new members is largely a fiction.

Nevertheless, the new members do not have an opt-out clause like the UK or Denmark, and membership should in principle force them to adopt convergent policies. Many of them have drawn the conclusion that it would be better to join the euro. The heterogeneity of the euro zone would increase considerably, with respect to growth, inflation and divergent business cycles. Moreover, the battles for influence between the board of the ECB and the national central banks over the day-to-day running of the system or over questions of international representation weaken the institution and handicap its ability to make decisions. Enlargement of the euro zone, which is likely to take place from 2006–7 onwards, according to the current timetable, promises to further dilute these responsibilities, and we run the risk of managing the currency on the basis of international diplomacy.

Finally the question of budgetary policy has to be asked. Will the EU be able to steer as many economic and budgetary policies as there are new Member States, given that it already has difficulties organizing co-operation between the current members?

Clarify the strategy of the ECB and reform its governance

As far as the ECB is concerned, we do not feel it is a matter of its mandate. While the Americans have given an equal weighting to monetary stability and growth, the Europeans have decided to give their central bank the narrow task of ensuring price stability. This choice, to which a growing number of countries around the world are subscribing,[11] is a product of our history, and a consequent aversion to inflation. It is also the result of the essential compromises of monetary union, notably for the German people, for whom monetary stability is one of the great gains of peace. There is no need to reopen the issue and to question the ECB mandate.

However, the monetary strategy of the Central Bank, its internal governance, and its relationship with its political and institutional environment may all be discussed:

- The monetary strategy adopted by the Central Bank (as opposed to actual decisions) has shown weaknesses. The two-'pillar' structure (money supply vs. price cost and exchange rate indicators) damages the clarity of monetary policy (if not its practice) since it is easy to justify any deviation from such an eclectic rule. Judging from experience, the numerical definition – a price increase between 0 and 2 per cent – by which the ECB has translated the treaty goal of price stability seems to be inappropriate. The very low level of the ceiling chosen by the ECB places it in a dilemma: either it does everything possible to respect its goal, to the detriment of intelligent management of the economic cycle, or – and this is what it has chosen – it has to endure persistent deviations above the upper band,[12] to the peril of its credibility. The viability of this rule will be even more doubtful after enlargement of the euro zone to transition countries, where rates of growth and inflation are necessarily higher.
- Decisions in the Council of governors of the Eurosystem are based on the principle of one person, one vote, with no distinction by nationality, and the search for consensus. With upcoming enlargement, Europe cannot take the risk of turning the ECB into a monetary UN. The Nice Treaty foresaw the possibility of reforming voting procedures, to avoid paralysis of decision-making. Three options could be considered: the delegation of power to a monetary policy committee made up of leading European figures; a combination of permanent seats for large countries' governors, and rotating seats for the others; or the creation of a system of constituencies, much as is found at the IMF. The first is certainly the closest in spirit to the institutions, although it is unclear whether the states are ready for it; the third is certainly the most remote.

- Owing to a lack of consideration when drafting the treaty, the way in which the Central Bank accounts for its actions has not received adequate attention. The ECB appears to wander between several alternative models in relation to its mandate. A direct face-to-face relationship with citizens, based on the German model, presupposes the existence of a public sphere, a high level of confidence in the institution and a clear consensus on the primacy of price stability. A second alternative would be a codified relationship with the political authorities, following the British model, coupled with more transparent communication with the market. Finally, a more French model could be followed, which could be based on an institutionalized dialogue with the political authorities (Eurogroup and Council). Faced with this choice, the Bank too often hides behind an intransigent defence of an independence that is not under threat, forgetting that in the long run its legitimacy rests on the quality of its performance as well as on its relationship with those who created it.
- Finally, the macroeconomic dialogue between representatives of the Council, the Parliament, the ECB, and social partners on the interaction between economic policy, monetary policy and wages that was initiated two years ago needs to be deepened. It is an opportunity for an important exchange of information and a chance for all players to learn the new rules of the European macroeconomic game. It would also be worth developing means of involving European civil society in discussions on macroeconomic and monetary perspectives.

We propose:

- *That the ECB abandon the two-pillar strategy, in favour of a symmetric target for inflation, expressed as a range of, say, 1 to 3 per cent.*

- *A reform of the governing body of the ECB, in order to preserve its ability to decide in anticipation of a wide enlargement. This reform should be done rapidly (it was already called for at Nice) and should reinforce the ECB board, whose role in decision-making and the dialogue with the political pillar (especially the Eurogroup) are essential.*
- *A clarification of the ECB's mandate and accountability procedures. In the absence of a system of operational independence based on the British model which would, for example, give the Eurogroup the right to set (on the basis of a Commission recommendation) the price inflation objective with complete transparency, and for a fixed period, we would suggest (a) that the definition of the objective is subject to prior consultation with other institutions and undergoes regular evaluations, and (b) the principles and means by which the ECB gives an account of its action to the Eurogroup, the European Parliament, and the public, are clarified. The system of open letters in cases of deviation from the goals could be adopted in this spirit, and an anonymous account of the debates of the Council of Governors could be published every quarter.*

Implementing economic policy coordination

From Maastricht to Amsterdam and the creation of the Eurogroup, the French left has championed the coordination of economic policies in the euro zone. The idea underpinning this project is very simple: for as long as the Member States do not envisage granting the EU a macroeconomically significant budget, in the manner of federal states, common budgetary action necessarily must rest on a coordination of national policies. This also applies to fields where instruments remain in the hands of states, but where there is a need for joint actions. A recent example was the allocation of third-generation mobile phone licences, which, owing to a lack of coordination, resulted in revenue for the states that plunged in first and in cross-border transfers between European consumers.[13]

The question is difficult for several reasons. First, the European Union cannot fall back on traditional methods in this matter. Its usual methods are harmonization (the fixing of common rules) and delegation (the transfer of responsibility to a EU authority). In the 1990s, convergence was added (the fixing of common goals). But coordination does not belong to this list. Second, there is no consensus on the need to coordinate economic policy in Europe. For many, the only coordination that is required is convergence on balanced budgets. Third, it is intrinsically difficult to coordinate decisions taken in the framework of disparate procedures and as a function of national political imperatives.

There has been some progress. The EU has set up the components required for coordination: namely, bodies (of which the Eurogroup is the main one), procedures, and the elements of a common doctrine. But the practice does not match the ambition. In the Eurogroup, governments do not play the game of coordination properly. That would require transparency, information sharing, and consulting other Member States on the direction of economic policy before announcing national decisions such as fiscal reforms. The Broad Economic Policy Guidelines, outlined in the treaty, are a little-known document, read only in EU circles, and to which neither governments nor national parliaments feel truly committed. The dialogue with the ECB is limited, because it refuses any commitment, even conditional. This, for example, prevents the Central Bank, when faced with an economic slowdown, from entering into an implicit contract with governments, under the terms of which it would support the economy as long as the states limited their deficits. As for the Commission, it tends to be wrapped up too often in a role of guardian of procedures, which certainly conforms to the treaty but is clearly insufficient.

This situation results in the policy mix of the euro zone being too often a simple *a posteriori* reading of what has been done, rather than the expression of a willingness to define *ex ante* an economic policy adapted to the whole of the euro zone. This situation is economically dangerous, because it risks depriving the zone of its capacity to react to external, and perhaps internal, difficulties. Economic policy does not boil down to a collection of disciplines and rules of good conduct. Like an autopilot, these might suffice most of the time, when it is calm or slightly rough. But there are times when it is necessary to have the ability to decide and act. The United States has shown us this. Faced with an unknown and changing situation, Europe cannot limit itself to applying rules, even if it does so intelligently.

In the longer term, coordination also implies structural policies. The European Central Bank makes no secret of the fact that it considers non-inflationary growth within the euro zone to lie between 2 and 2.5 per cent. At Lisbon governments agreed on a goal of growth in the order of 3 per cent, with a view to full employment. This quantitative gap signals a basic divergence between what governments hope for and what the ECB thinks is realistic today. The Central Bank's assessment is that government reform efforts are insufficient, and it thinks that without them unemployment cannot fall by much without inducing wage pressures. It considers that structural reforms are needed for Europe to enjoy the gains in productivity that the United States had in the second half of the 1990s; and as it holds monetary power, it is in a position to block growth that it feels would cause inflationary pressures.

The only response to this dilemma is a dialogue between governments and the ECB on the evaluation of the economic situation, inflationary risks and the impact of structural measures on the potential for growth and lowering of unemployment. It is thus essential to open a structured and meaningful dialogue – which implies that governments agree to listen to the ECB's criticisms, and that the ECB accepts that they will evaluate its appraisals of the risks to price stability, and critically if necessary. It is under these conditions that the euro zone could put in place the combination of macroeconomic and structural policies needed to achieve the goal of full employment.

The situation is also dangerous from a political point of view, because the response that the euro zone does or does not make to growing international risks will be seen as a test by the public. The euro has long been presented to them as a shield. Just as they are getting used to the notes and coins, this test will make them decide if the instrument is up to the job. If the euro comes across as badly managed, disciplined but without a project, then its legitimacy will be called into question.

Proposals have been made over the past few months, on the basis of which some immediate progress could be achieved, if the Member States wish it.[14] Further progress, which would require negotiations and, eventually, treaty amendments, will only be possible in the longer run.

We propose:

- *The definition of principles of economic policy for the euro zone that would go beyond budgetary discipline. These would detail how to use economic policy instruments in times of unexpected shocks, and discuss the proper management of budgetary policy in order that it retain its role as an instrument of national economic policy.*
- *A discussion of fiscal discipline in a medium to long-term perspective. This would give priority to dealing with debt levels and take into account investment need and the governments' implicit liabilities.*
- *A regular examination by the Eurogroup of the policy mix and the structural policies of the euro zone taken as a whole, which would serve as a basis for the definition of economic policy guidelines for the entire zone.*

- *A reciprocal and binding engagement of euro zone Member States to consult their partners and the Commission before any substantial decision on economic policy.*
- *In the framework of budget discussions, a systematic debate by each national parliament on the broad directions of economic policy in the euro zone.*
- *A strengthening of the Eurogroup, with (a) instead of a rotating presidency, a president designated for a fixed period and confirmed by the European Parliament, capable of representing the euro zone internationally; (b) a permanent secretariat within the Commission; and (c) a capacity to vote by qualified majority on the guidelines for economic policy suggested by the Commission for the entire euro zone.*

A balanced single market

The single market is one of the European Union's great achievements. But it is incomplete in two respects. First, integration has not been achieved in certain sectors, partly owing to French reluctance. Second, and more importantly, the freeing of barriers to trade happened much more quickly than the establishment of regulation in the European market. The pursuit of integration is necessary because it brings economic advantages – as seen with the liberalization of telecommunications, which has already allowed a fall in prices – and because it lowers the risk of the single market falling apart after enlargement. But integration by liberalization should be accompanied by clear rules that protect the European model. The Commission has begun a discussion on services of general economic interest, which should be deepened in the search for a healthy balance between openness and regulation.

The financial sector is a clear representation of this state of affairs. The decompartmentalization of markets has rapidly increased over the past few years, and integration of banking should follow after a phase of consolidation at the national level. But the dispersal of bodies charged with banking supervision and the surveillance of financial markets continues. For as long as decentralization kept the advantage of proximity, not integrating those authorities was justified. Now, it has become risky not to integrate them.

The question of taxes should be seen in this light. Tax harmonization is not an end in itself and it is natural that the EU's Member States keep the essentials of their fiscal autonomy, as they do not make the same choices with regard to the divisions between public and private, the provision of services, or aid and redistribution. It should be recalled that in spite of the progress in integration, there has not been any convergence in the EU in levels of public expenditure, and this spread is bound to increase with enlargement. This fiscal autonomy results in competition between states for the provision of high-quality services at the best prices. This competition is part of the game and there is no reason to reject it when it deals not with levels of expenditure or tax but with the quality/price relationship, that is to say the efficiency of the public sphere.

However, it is necessary to neutralize fiscal competition when it is not properly used and so damages efficiency. This goes for taxes on savings – see the decisions of the Feira European Council, which fixed the goal of a general exchange of information in this respect. The fact that the goal is far off, that there is room for caution (and that there were many delaying tactics) should not hide the fact that the goal itself is legitimate. The same applies to the question of corporate taxation: the heterogeneity of tax regimes is a cost for businesses, a distorting factor in investment decisions and, for multinationals, an opportunity to avoid taxation which the removal of exchange-rate costs will only increase. Disparities in taxation levels can be criticized when they no longer reflect the different choices about the level of public expenditure, but rather fiscal competition to attract a mobile factor (capital) to the detriment of a fixed factor (labour). That justifies at least creating a minimum rate of effective corporate tax, and then to go further towards a European corporate tax, whose proceeds would be either given to the EU budget, or divided between the Member States.

We propose:

- *moving to qualified majority voting for all fiscal decision-making related to the single market;*
- *the harmonization of tax regimes on businesses and the establishment of a minimum rate of corporate tax, leading in steps towards a European business tax;*
- *establishing a single financial market regulator and starting a process of unified banking supervision.*

Betting on sustainable development

Economic policy cannot be limited to the short-term support of growth and employment. It must become increasingly concerned with the preservation of the future and must deal with collective objectives outside the economic field. There are many diverse challenges, including the preservation of the environment and natural resources, the long-term sustainability of economic policies (whether the anticipation of future financial risks or the consolidation of pension systems), risk management, access for all to knowledge and to technology. All these issues are gradually becoming more important in people's minds, and could be categorized under the generic term of 'sustainable development'. Often these preoccupations lead to an intergenerational perspective on economic and social policy.

Viewed from such a perspective, the European level is frequently seen as the most pertinent for effective action. This is certainly the case when these issues have a continental or global dimension: the capacity to negotiate the international management of global public goods (greenhouse gases, for example); to limit the risks linked with maritime transport or food safety; or to create infrastructures that respect the environment (rail). But it is also often the case when the individual action of each country could support common initiatives: everyone can build the 'information society' in their own way, but the impact of these efforts would be of greater importance if Europe could produce an original model for the control and diffusion of digital technology.

Supporting the fight for the environment

The importance of the environmental challenge is not a controversial question. The scientific diagnosis of the risks for the climate and the environment more generally can no longer be questioned, and future generations will ask us to explain our actions. Public opinion in Europe is reacting with increasing vigour to environmental degradation and threats to health (cruelly recalled by recent accidents). In contrast, the pursuit of environmental objectives can play a dynamic role in the logic of growth, development and social well-being. At the same time, it is becoming ever clearer that when individual profit maximization ignores environmental damage it carries much of the blame for upsetting the ecological balance. The battle for sustainable development naturally fits into the European left's programme in their attempt to regulate capitalism.

The subject is one of those on which Europeans have common collective preferences that distinguish them from other continents or groups of countries. Their level of income contributes to the value they attribute to the protection of the environment. The population density, the diversity of landscapes, and a persistent rural element all make our citizens particularly sensitive to their quality of life. Thus there is a specific European vision of the environmental challenges, which expresses itself in international negotiations as it does in the choices of internal development.

Europe reduced its greenhouse gas emissions by 4 per cent between 1990 and 1999, but it will have to redouble its efforts to reach the 8 per cent reduction by 2010 (relative to 1990) agreed at Kyoto. The question goes beyond the purely ecological field. In order to achieve the goals laid out in the Kyoto Protocol, there will have to be purposeful actions in sectors such as energy, transport, agriculture, trade and development aid. In transport, there will have to be a real effort to control the growth of traffic flows, but up until now governments have been timid, doubtless because of the way in which lobby groups have mobilized. Agriculture must also make a contribution, given that it is the source of 12 to 15 per cent of greenhouse gas emissions. More generally, implementing a tax system that encourages modes of production and consumption which use less energy should, along with the creation of a market for trading greenhouse gas emission credits, allow us to achieve these objectives.

Europe, having placed the precautionary principle among the EU's norms, could be a leader, even if it has yet to get that principle completely accepted internationally. The environmental *acquis communautaire* addresses the reduction of pollution through tax incentives, by encouraging environmental responsibility, and through the control of state aids under competition policy.

Thus it is possible to define a common global goal, laying the foundations for sustainable development in Europe, in the space of a generation, with intermediate quantitative goals and an annual evaluation. Environmental action should aim to create growth that has no negative environmental effects. The European Union should present its main contributions at the follow-up to the Rio Conference, at Johannesburg in 2002. At the European level itself, the EU's procedures should take more notice of the dimensions of sustainable development.

Four levels of instruments can be envisaged:

- *Environmental norms* (air pollution, waste, recycling) should be gradually raised, following a timetable agreed beforehand so that businesses can make the necessary investment.
- *Incentives* such as the use of best practices, frameworks for state aid, procedures for public contracting, the allocation of structural funds and farming aid, and projects financed by the EIB.
- *The basis of a European tax system* should be put in place. The creation of a European tax (which would replace the French tax on pollution) would have the double effect of fostering the integration of citizens and financing a policy of sustainable development in Europe: one naturally thinks of the eternally postponed efforts on rail-freight, as well as support for renewable energy. This ecological tax would be the European Union's contribution towards a larger and longer-term plan on the international level.
- *Economic instruments* that facilitate changes in the modes of production while maintaining economic efficiency.

A programme for sustainable growth

In March 2000, at the Lisbon European Council, the Fifteen agreed an ambitious agenda designed to 'put in place the infrastructure necessary for diffusing knowledge, reinforcing innovation and economic reform, and modernizing social security and education systems'. The challenge was to define a unified strategy for the transition to the information economy, by promoting new technologies and business creation, enhancing the internal market and the sustainability of economic policies, as well as social cohesion, higher levels of employment,[15] and investment in training.

A set of indicators quantifying the performance of Member States in growth, innovation, employment, as well as social cohesion and the environment, were developed to facilitate the discussion. All these issues, including the environment, are to be the subject of a spring meeting of the European Council.

To recap, the Lisbon agenda sought to bring Europe's potential development up to that of the United States, without sacrificing its social model. It has been criticized for often contradictory reasons: by liberals who are sceptical in principle, sometimes to the point of caricature, as to Europe's ability to rival the United States economically; and by the left, who fear that market liberalization will predominate, even though the social element of the process remains imprecise and lacks concrete instruments.

This fear is legitimate: it is true that the summits at Lisbon and then Stockholm were viewed as a forum for France to oppose its more liberal partners (the UK and Spain in particular) on the opening of competition in the areas of gas, electricity and transport, and as an opportunity for the Commission to recall its grievances on the transposition of directives and the reduction of state aids, rather than as the scene of political debate on the conditions of economic and social development in Europe. In particular, how we preserve public services from the competition of network industries has not yet been properly addressed.

The merits of the Lisbon programme should not, however, be forgotten. After ten years marked by budgetary adjustments, Lisbon was the visible expression of movement towards goals of growth, employment and social cohesion. It is the only example of a coherent European economic and social strategy, discussed at the highest political level, and articulated around simple goals that Europeans can easily understand. The weighting of the different elements in the programme – notably between liberalization and regulation – are naturally the source of debate between different European viewpoints. But the Lisbon process creates a space for just such a debate. It allows for the reintroduction of political decision-making when it is necessary to trade off different objectives, avoiding the balkanization of decision-making that might stem from the lack of a final objective, and thus prevent the norms of the internal market and competition from gaining a position of absolute power. It should be upgraded, just as an effort should be made to keep a balanced approach, so that it does not become a simple agenda for deepening the single market.

Thus it is wrong to identify Europe as an engine for liberalization. If the creation of the single market necessarily required challenging a certain number of national monopolies and often protectionist regulations, new forms of regulation have been created through a series of independent national authorities that protect against discrimination and ensure transparency and the respect for public service obligations. This is the case for sectors such as telecommunications and energy – where national regulators have the task of fixing market rules, with regard to price and network access – or transport, where the authorities regulate the allocation of landing slots for airlines and track space for rail companies. It has, however, become necessary to coordinate the actions of these regulators, who have, without asking for authorization, already developed the habit of meeting each other.

To have any weight in these debates and put forward its ideas on regulation, France must abandon its (too-often) defensive posture. Its reluctance toward the creation of a single market in energy or transport, when the benefits of such integration are at least as great as the trade in goods, prevent it from being influential in the key debates on the structures of regulation necessary to ensure the proper functioning of the markets, the security of energy supplies in Europe, the protection of the environment and consumers, and equity between citizens. It is not important to know how quickly the markets will integrate and liberalize: they are already doing so. Nor it is important to know if Électricité de France and Gaz de France will adapt to this: they are already doing so. What is important is to know if this will bring about a system which makes liberalization an end in itself, or will lead to a vision that puts collective goals and the necessary structures of public regulation before that.

We propose:

- *An active commitment by France to the realization of a single market for energy and services. This engagement should be accompanied by propositions for regulation, with a view to putting these markets at the service of collective goals.*
- *The creation of a European tax on energy sources, in proportions to be determined relative to the consumption of energy and their carbon content. Its level could be fixed at €75 per tonne of carbon in 2010, as it is for the French greenhouse gas programme.*
- *Using some of this eco-tax for a European plan to develop transport systems that respect the environment (rail-freight), notably to accompany the creation of infrastructures in the new Member States.*
- *A redressing of the balance of the springtime European Councils devoted to economic and social questions, in order better to integrate the goals of employment, social cohesion and the development of services of general economic interest, so that the EU will have an inter-sectoral arbitration designed to match the objectives it has set itself.*

Bring social Europe to life

From the left's perspective, European integration can appear fundamentally unbalanced. There are, therefore, many who call for 'the social' to match the economic. This demand is understandable in the framework of looking for a middle-ground in Europe. It is even more so now that we can expect a reinforcing of competition, as was noted above, on the macroeconomic as well as the structural level. This economic movement should be accompanied and balanced by a wider social dialogue, if Europe is not to run the risk of a growing imbalance between the social and the economic, which could lead to the creation of a market society. This unacceptable development can only be avoided by the construction of a Social Europe that accompanies economic integration. The difficulty of this task lies in the uncertainty about its foundations and instruments. Therefore, we need to be clear about both of these, before describing what they can achieve.

The foundations

Without wishing to oversimplify the matter, social Europe has three foundations that it is necessary to distinguish:

- The first is the willingness to *regulate competition*. Member States have decided to exclude communal social norms from the field of comparative advantage. Health and safety in the workplace, professional equality between women and men, working time, etc. The goal is to limit the social effects of competitive pressures. To a significant extent, wages and wage costs do not fall into this category today: we accept competition on prices and wages. But we could expect that in the perspective of convergence, with the progression of integration and higher worker mobility, the notion of a European minimum wage will end up making sense.
- The second relates to the *integration of markets for labour and firms*. This primarily includes everything linked to the mobility of people, and in particular workers. To make freedom of movement, one of the founding principles of the EU, more than just a theoretical right, a range of social requirements should be drafted so that individuals retain the security offered by their national social provisions. The next step is to address the right of workers in multinationals to make themselves heard at the level where economic decisions are made.

125

- The third is the *existence of a common identity*, which should be allowed both to exist and to be renewed in a world of rapid change. The challenge here is the size of the project, rather than harmonization or legislation. It requires knowing, for example, how to respond to new challenges that arise from economic insecurity, even precariousness; long-term unemployment; inequality; the need for lifelong learning, etc. These challenges are more or less common to all. The survival of a European social identity fundamentally depends on our ability to respond to them together, since it is illusory to think that each country can build an alternative to the American model on its own. But the instruments used to achieve these ends do not necessarily need to be harmonized.

A basic set of norms, conditions of integration, and the renewal of our social identity: it is through these three measures that we must assess the path we have travelled. It is more important than a point-by-point comparison between the economic and social would suggest. In the European firm, in the European sphere, there is the best level of protection in the world, the best dialogue. But it remains incomplete, and enlargement, which will significantly increase the EU's diversity, might well lead to hard debates on social questions.

Enlarge the foundation of common norms

On the first of these foundations progress has been slow and difficult, but since the adoption in 1989 of the Social Charter and legislative texts (notably on health and safety at work), a body of rules has been developed, without equal in the rest of the world. Progress has also been made on the method. Since the Social Protocol of Maastricht, which was incorporated into the Treaty of Amsterdam, we have moved on from simple exchanges of points of view, which only resulted in the adoption of common opinions where there was convergence. There is now recognition of the role of social partners in producing EU regulation, but also in the affirmation of the predominance of conventions over legislation. It was on this basis that framework agreements could be drafted on parental leave (1996) and part-time work (1997), and then be enlarged, *erga omnes*, by means of an EU directive. From these first successes there followed the stalemate of negotiations on temporary work, but the recent opening of a negotiation on tele-working offers the opportunity to begin the work again.

The definition of possible progress needs to take into account enlargement, which will cause a marked increase in the disparities of development across the EU. That will prevent any short-term development in the fixing of quantitative common norms, for example with regard to minimum wage, working hours, or the requirements of professional training: such norms will inevitably be too high for some and too low for others. Instead, it is necessary to make progress on the principles and procedural guarantees. Precisely because the EU is going to enlarge, it is necessary for the rules of the game, upon which the members agree, to be reaffirmed, and it should be clearly reiterated that workers will benefit from a minimum wage and collective guarantees as well as the exercise of their social rights within the firm.

It is also important to guarantee the effective implementation of EU social legislation. What use is there, for example, in legislating on health and safety in the workplace, if the measures are not properly applied – especially by SMEs? This question will clearly come up more pointedly with enlargement. Control and assistance will take on an increasing importance.

Accompany economic integration

The free movement of people and the conditions to undertake professional activities in another European country are often seen as the preoccupations of the privileged. This is a mistake, because there are ever more young people, not necessarily highly qualified, whose work or search for work takes them across borders. But a young unemployed French worker who returns from having worked in a call centre in Ireland receives only three months of unemployment benefits at the Irish rate upon his return. Obsessed by the idea that it is necessary to discourage 'social tourism', Europeans have neglected the social rights of mobile workers.[16] It is time to reopen this debate, not to promote the international mobility of workers, but to ensure that these developments do not take place to the detriment of workers. The objective should be to guarantee the equality of rights between resident workers and mobile workers.

The representation of workers in multinational companies has been on hold for a long time, but recent advances have been made, notably regarding European Works Councils (1994) and the participation of workers in European companies (2000). These developments need to be secured in practice. There is also room for examining with the European social partners, under a procedure foreseen by the treaty, where it is possible to open sectoral discussions on wages. The potential usefulness of such discussions varies from one sector to another, but in some sectors the question of such a parallelism has already been posed, and this can only gain in importance with the introduction of the euro.

Revitalize our social model

Above all else, it is necessary to know what we want from our model. Its renewal cannot happen without the active participation of civil society, and especially social partners, who are not listened to enough today. This project should be based on our values, which are those of social democracy. It should take into account the *acquis*, which is primarily rooted in the field of social protection. It should base itself on the instruments of social dialogue, notably through the Economic and Social Councils, which should be restructured in order to play their role.

The efforts of the last few years have not led to the rejuvenation of the European model, but instead to the coordination of social policies, in particular through the introduction of an 'employment' title in the Amsterdam Treaty, the elaboration of National Action Plans for employment and the adoption, under the Portuguese Presidency, of what is called the 'open method of coordination'.

There is a certain ambiguity to this approach. Sceptics point out the often formal character of the coordination exercise – which sometimes is little more than a presentation of measures that have already been decided upon – and the risk that the open method of coordination will serve as a pretext for downgrading legislative harmonization. Others find virtue in an approach which uses benchmarks, as in businesses, as it forces each country to compare itself to others on the basis of quantitative indicators. Coordination, even if non-binding, mobilizes convergence around those practices which have been successful, and encourages each country to improve its social policies. As it is based on experience and the comparison of experiences, it favours the emergence of workable solutions.

To avoid confusion and temptation to dilute social ambitions, the field of open coordination needs to be precisely delimited. With this condition, it is useful that the Member States confront their experiences and reflect together on the renewal of their social model. In effect, everyone faces the same problems, such as social exclusion, changing work conditions, rising economic insecurity, the need for lifelong learning, ageing populations and the balancing of pension systems. To respond to these problems, there needs to be the definition of new procedures, new instruments and new social rights. As it is difficult to harmonize what already exists, it might be easier to find common solutions to emerging problems. It is, as a priority, these challenges that the coordination of social policies should focus on.

We propose:

- *Adding to the base of common social norms the principle of a minimum wage and a minimum income, defined in real terms, but whose levels would be a function of the general economic development of each country. However, given the different levels of development, we have to exclude for the medium term the fixing of a common minimum wage for the EU as a whole.*
- *Transcribing into positive law, and integrating into the common norms, the principles adopted at Nice in the Charter of Fundamental Rights (information and consultation of workers, collective negotiation and action, protection against unfair dismissal, working conditions, etc.).*
- *Reopening the debate on the construction of a set of social rights for mobile workers, with a view to improving definitions of the conditions for accessing and maintaining these rights, and to ensure the equality of rights between resident workers and mobile workers.*
- *Drafting a European work contract, that is, defining for all the countries of the EU the minimum conditions which such a contract should meet; other conditions and specific clauses in different countries, and possibly in different sectors, could then be added.*

Reform the CAP

Pioneer of common policies, and the symbol of EU solidarity with a rural economy facing profound changes, the Common Agricultural Policy has become an impediment to European integration. It is a symbol of the endless race to higher productivity, favouring the modes of production held responsible for both health crises and environmental degradation. These criticisms are joined by more traditional ones, which have for many years denounced the costly and bureaucratic interventions that mainly benefit those farmers and regions which are the most comfortable, especially in France. They reinforce the positions of our trade partners, both the Americans and those emerging or developing countries who, as the Doha discussions demonstrated, want to place agriculture inside international trade law. They could place France in a very uncomfortable position at a moment of crucial decisions on enlargement.

A policy of the past

Constantly being remodelled, and on the eve of further re-examination due in 2002–3 (just as the 1999 reforms come into force), the CAP is not able to offer stable rules to farmers who are less and less happy with the calling into question of the system. In its current form, the CAP handicaps Europe in both the preparation of enlargement and multilateral negotiations, it discredits us in the eyes of developing countries and it weakens the European will to regulate globalization. The changes begun by the reforms of 1992 and then 1999, with the shift from price support to direct aid, has not resolved the lack of legitimacy from which it suffers. Indeed, quite the opposite. It has highlighted this problem by rendering such support, and the unfairness of its allocation, all the more visible. But as the CAP is called into question, this in turn affects public opinion in the two co-founders of this common policy: France (recipient 23 per cent of European support) and Germany (14 per cent). It has weakened the system of joint management of public authorities and the mainstream farming unions, which was an element of political and social control by the farming community during the years of change, but which is now ill-suited to addressing the interests of other players: non-mainstream unions, consumers, those concerned about the environment, and non-farming rural dwellers.

Recent events have changed the scene decisively. As a result of the BSE crisis, Germany recently began a radical shake-up of its agricultural policy. While in the past Germany had opposed lower guaranteed prices under the pressure of a particularly powerful farming lobby, Chancellor Schröder did denounce the principle of joint management and gave priority to the defence of consumers. The SPD–Green government coalition is torn between a reorientation of the CAP, such as that proposed by the French government since 1997 with the extension of the agricultural guidance law, and a radical abandonment of any European agricultural policy. In the context of enlargement, French stubbornness could push it towards the second option.

As the re-examination of the CAP approaches, coinciding with the last phase of enlargement negotiations and, in 2003, with the active phase of WTO agricultural negotiations under the timetable agreed at Doha, the temptation exists – even among some parts of the European left – to return to the market and abandon public intervention. Faced with what resembles a European front against the CAP, France and Ireland are isolated in their desire to safeguard the *acquis* of the Common Agricultural Policy. But to enter into negotiations with a defensive posture would not only be politically costly, as was the case during the Berlin negotiations in 1999: it would be to risk a major setback. Defence of the CAP such as we know it now runs against the interests of French agriculture and, more generally, against the economic interests of the country.

France should thus proceed with a cool re-examination of its agricultural priorities, without taboos, and clarify the coherence of its position on the CAP with regard to the internal restructuring it initiated in 1999. For example, it does not necessarily hold true that in an enlarging Europe an agriculture system that increasingly values quality and product differentiation, including differentiation according to origin, should continue to be managed at the EU level, even if a renationalization of direct market aids, which would damage the internal market, remains unacceptable. Nor does it necessarily hold that the current means of supporting agriculture allows France to make the most of its comparative advantage in the face of countries less well endowed than itself. As for the 'mission to export' of European or French agriculture, it no longer exists for other products. It cannot be anything other than the result of production that is competitive in quality and price.

A deep reform of agricultural policy

The specificities of agriculture justify public intervention on the grounds of public health, preservation of the environment, and the management of Europe's territory – i.e. because of the cultural element of food products. These are the contours of a renovated agricultural policy, capable of gaining much support from European public opinion – including farmers. In this spirit, France, the principal beneficiary and inspiration for the CAP, should take the initiative in suggesting to its partners (and particularly Germany) a new basic European pact. The main aims of such a reform plan would be:

- To respond to the worries of Europeans about the security and the quality of their food, the preservation of the environment, and the management of territory. The new common agricultural policy should encourage modes of production that respond to these worries, turning its back on 'commercialization'.
- To design a stable long-term perspective for farmers and the rural community, who cannot simply limit themselves to welcoming people from the cities.
- To maintain the single market.
- To create the conditions for the success of a broad enlargement, and to favour a new European consensus which involves the new Member States.

- To contribute to the solution of the EU's budgetary problems, including those which concern the major contributing states and the reduction of the British contribution, which no longer makes any sense.
- To place it in the framework of international trade.

This leads us to imagine a renovated CAP based, in the long run, on three elements: (a) aid linked to production (market aids), of which the division between sectors deserves to be re-examined. (Export refunds have already become a thing of the past for some cereals: discussion should follow on adapting this tool to the needs of animal production.) (b) a rural development mechanism; (c) food security.

Even with updated means, today's CAP is based almost exclusively on the first of these (only 10 per cent of CAP funds are devoted to rural development; food security is completely absent).

The objective for the next five years would be, for example, to devote about 40 per cent of the CAP's resources to help develop the rural sphere, using new means that would give a single payment for each hectare completely decoupled from production, available to all (except milk farmers, who receive quotas). This aid would be limited according to the type of utilization and subject to environmental conditionality. In this framework, it could be accompanied by a bonus for certain types of use (vegetable protein, bio-farming, etc.). It would be the object of co-financing region by region since, as it would be decoupled from production, it would not damage the single market.

The financial means needed would be found through the redeployment of budgets currently devoted to direct aids, which could be reduced by 5 per cent every year, steadily decreasing each year. Two-thirds of the funds freed could be used for the enhancement of the rural environment, and one-third for food safety. The shift from price support to direct aid was a necessary first step, but the validity of a reference to past prices and production, upon which this aid is calculated, has been eroded over time. It would be better to focus instead on long-term rural development.

Finally, an effort in the direction of food quality and safety would meet the worries of consumers. It should be conducted in part at the EU level, if we do not want to create a contradiction between the logic of the single market and that of consumer protection. The means could include making direct aid and rural development subject to conditions on food quality, or the encouragement of techniques that improve safety.

We propose:

- *accelerating the development of rural development policies at the expense of direct market aids, with the goal of tripling CAP expenditure devoted to it over the next five years;*
- *as a result, reducing the means available to direct aid, by both progressively reducing it and reallocating it towards rural development;*
- *setting a hectare aid conditional on rural development policies, subject to strong and clear environmental conditions, as well as regionally managed bonuses for certain activities or modes of production (eco-farming, vegetable proteins etc.);*
- *endowing the CAP with a third section devoted to food security and quality;*
- *on this basis, elaborating a lasting solution to the budgetary problem of the EU, ending the special treatment from which the British benefit, as well as the claims of net contributors.*

Building a judicial space

The European Union wants a space within which its citizens can come and go freely. The dream is as old as the EU, but it has yet to be achieved. Firstly, because while there is freedom of movement, the right of establishment remains incomplete: for example, an unemployed person does not have the right to leave his or her country to find work in another Member State. Freedom of establishment raises questions of property law, labour law, and fiscal and social rights, some of which issues have already been mentioned. But freedom of movement also implies certain guarantees: which translates into the objective of building an 'integrated sphere of freedom, security and justice', as the EU has agreed.

The goal is still far from being achieved. Of 375 million Europeans, only 5.5 million (or 1.5 per cent) live in an EU country of which they are not nationals. The problem of rights of guardianship and access visits for dual-national divorcees still has not been resolved, without even mentioning the transfer of pensions, and family conflicts. And we know, thanks to the Geneva appeal of instructing magistrates, that while the free circulation of transnational crime has developed considerably, along with its products (such as drugs and counterfeit goods), those who support it, and the capital that it produces, the magistrates charged with tracking them down remain largely confined within their national frontiers. The extradition of criminals remains a long, complex and uncertain procedure.

Limited progress

This lack of balance is shocking, because it goes against our initial ambitions and once again highlights the prioritization of economic integration. This began to be corrected with the Maastricht Treaty, whose 'third pillar' foresaw the reinforcement of external controls in the fields of asylum, visas and immigration, civil judicial co-operation, police co-operation, and criminal judicial co-operation. The Schengen Convention simultaneously organized the removal of barriers between the signatory states.

Since then, the third pillar has moved forward much more quickly than was expected immediately after Maastricht. The Amsterdam

Treaty brought an extension of the Schengen sphere to the whole EU, and a move to qualified majority voting on its associated provisions, which should begin in 2004. The move to a community – rather than a strictly intergovernmental – regime for visas, asylum, immigration and civil judicial co-operation (in so far as it concerns the free movement of people) is also in sight. As for criminal co-operation, it has given rise to several important initiatives: the development of an operational capacity and autonomous investigations by Europol; the implementation of Eurojust (at Nice) with a view to instituting permanent co-operation between criminal judicial systems; and a limited simplification of extradition procedures.[17]

Measured against what was foreseen a few years ago, these advances have been impressive, but compared to the expectations of citizens, they remain very weak. Moreover, the Member States' positions on immigration are often incoherent, resulting in a spiral of restrictive national practices that is detrimental to both the elaboration of minimum requirements for immigration (leading to clandestine immigration) and the proper treatment of foreigners with regular positions. The dramatic rise in clandestine passengers to England repeatedly illustrates the point.

Take the opportunity to move forward

The mobilization that followed the attacks of 11 September offers the opportunity to move forward and establish a European judicial sphere, and to accept that 'what is decided by a judge in one state should be recognized in another', to use the formula of the president of the Court of Justice, Carlos Iglesias.

As regards issues relating to welcoming foreigners (visas, asylum, immigration), the objectives should be the adoption of common lines on immigration, based on indicative goals, an active common policy of welcoming students and foreign researchers – which is important if Europe is to wield influence – and the adoption of a European statute for legal long-term migrants.

In the field of civil law, possible areas of progress include the early implementation of the regulation on the resolution of family conflicts (designation of competent courts, mutual recognition of judgments), and the introduction of a 'European executory title', guaranteeing the execution of judgments throughout the EU's territory.

In the field of criminal law, the new Eurojust could be used to harmonize rules of procedure (a European statement of cross-examination, a European arrest warrant, European rights of defence, a European statute for victims), in order to allow the removal of a formal extradition procedure, and so as to ensure the execution of decisions across the entire EU. It is also necessary to give Eurojust the possibility of ordering and coordinating enquiries (and not just to be informed), with the participation, under its control, of officers of Europol and agents of the Anti-Fraud Office (OLAF).

Finally, it must be remembered that the fight against money laundering remains a priority, and insufficient progress has been made here. We need a unified policy of prevention with respect to non-co-operative territories, and the unification of criminal law on the repression of trafficking dirty money across the EU.

We propose:

- *granting Europol a capacity to investigate;*
- *evolving Eurojust into a European public prosecutor's office, by granting it the power to start investigations into international offences;*
- *introducing the principle of mutual recognition of judicial decisions into the treaty;*
- *granting the EU the power to conclude international co-operation agreements with third countries in these fields.*

Make the EU an international player

What once motivated Member States, what drove integration forward, was the desire to build a new future together, to continue to exist in a world dominated by two giants who had divided Europe. For some, and particularly for France, it was also about having influence in the world. This plan was gradually incorporated into a proper foreign policy, but one which has made only rather timid advances.

This common foreign policy remains embryonic, lacking a real 'road map' based on a shared vision of Europe's role in the world. The stultifying search for the lowest common denominator predominates: usually, a defence of human rights, an indispensable goal but all the more insufficient because it does not differentiate us from our partners. Moreover, because of the lack of consensus on influencing events from start to finish, the EU is often limited to making purposeless declarations.

We should not be surprised by this as it relates, in foreign-policy terms, to the identity of each Member State: its vision of the world, the values that it holds and projects. Inevitably there are difficulties – when Member States aspire to project anything other than a variant of the American viewpoint or of purely mercantile interests. This situation is particularly painful for France, since its diplomacy is an attribute of power, of influence and of stature – and also a balancing element to the economic assets of Germany.

However, a common foreign and security policy should, more than ever, be at the centre of the European project of the French left. Why? Because to move in the direction of European integration is also to give oneself the means to have influence in the world and affirm an autonomous model of Europe that prioritizes sustainable development, security, the resolution of regional conflicts through the rights of people and individuals, and globalization with a human face. Faced with global challenges, Europe seems to be in a better position to act than individual Member States. Faced with threats to security, there is a strong demand for the construction of a common foreign and security policy.

It is necessary, however, to be aware of these difficulties and to adopt a gradual approach, firstly by privileging the ability of a united Europe to regulate globalization and establish the basis of a new North–South relationship.

A mixed assessment

The launch of a more ambitious EU foreign policy at Maastricht has brought only disappointment. The definition of common strategies has not led to concrete results, and the EU has long been handicapped, for example, by the difficulties it has experienced in intervening in the Balkan conflicts, or in playing an independent role in the Middle East – despite late but genuine progress before 11 September, on the Israeli–Palestinian conflict. The foreign policy of the EU still does not have a clearly defined strategy – either with regard to its geographical priorities, beyond an effort to foster its relationships with its neighbours following the Balkan wars; or in relation to its policy instruments, or, even less so, its organization. Europe, as far as foreign and security policy is concerned, lacks a global project.

In the economic domain the balance is more positive, even if incomplete. Europe exists as a commercial power, an actor that has the power to negotiate, and which can thus influence the direction of multilateral discussions. The Doha negotiations confirmed this by creating the conditions for new multilateral rules in globalization, beyond opening markets. It was a unified Europe that placed the preservation of the environment onto the agenda of the next round of multilateral trade negotiations, even if it failed to do the same for core labour standards. Not without difficulties, and at the price of having to compromise in places, it has used the issue of greenhouse gases to build a position distinct from that of the United States and to put in place the elements of a global accord that opens the way, if Russia confirms its commitment, to the entry into force of the Kyoto Protocol. Even if it is far from playing the leading role, it has been able, on occasions, to formulate ideas on the reform of the international financial architecture. However, co-operation between Member States suffers both because it is not based on a shared vision of strategic interests – including, and above all, the governance of globalization – and because it does not have the means for effective common action. Too often, the EU appears to give the impression that it refuses to define its objectives, and is content to intervene at the margins, trying to bend the American approach.

It is in the field of defence that the most notable progress has been made in the last few years. From the launch of a Franco-British initiative at St Malo in December 1998, a European defence initiative has rapidly taken shape. Certainly, the objectives of the European Policy of Security and Defence (EPSD) are modest. It is not about territorial defence, which remains with the Atlantic alliance, nor is it a step to a European army. The delegated tasks of European defence are restricted to humanitarian missions, crisis management, and the maintenance or re-establishment of peace. Clearly, its means also remain limited. And there is reason to fear a retreat after 11 September. But it is true that the problems of the complementarity of action between Europe and the Atlantic alliance have been resolved with the recognition by the latter of the European security and defence identity, and the acknowledgement that the EU has the right to use certain NATO resources. The Member States are determined to put into place a rapid reaction force of at least 60,000 troops from 2003, and to create the political and military tools needed for its control. Despite some problems with equipment, the implementation of this programme is running smoothly. This step forward provides the basis for further develements, notably with regard to the coordination of armament programmes and the integration of defence industries.

What remains to be invented is a common vision of the world and the manner in which we can have a real influence on its evolution. And not simply through declarations of principle or funding whose use is for other partners to serve their own political ends.

With regard to this objective, the impact of the entry of a dozen new Member States appears to be a major uncertainty. Will their desire to influence the international scene be strong? Was their plan for extracting themselves from the Soviet experience not simply to open up to the world, and gain the protection of the Americans through NATO? Will the sensitiveness of their populations to the effects of globalization be as great, with the support they expect from a stronger EU international presence? The absence of a colonial past exonerates the new Member States from the guilty consciences of the old colonial powers and could influence their attitude towards developing countries. Will that result in a greater priority on relations with close neighbours (the Balkans, Russia, the Middle East)? The fundamental question of Europe's borders is thus raised, as well as the definition of its new geopolitics.

A 'road map' for Europe in the world

To give Europe its own project in the world: such should be our ambition. No field of foreign and security policy should escape this démarche. And above all, not one which is at the heart of diplomatic activity: the political relationships with our major partners: the Americans, the Russians, and the developing world in all its diversity. From this point of view, there is also the question of European representation in the Security Council of the United Nations. But we need to take into account the difficulty of the task, the necessary transition, before the Europeans develop a common vision of the world and their contribution to it.

To this end, Europe should first of all take as a common road map the governance of globalization, notably in North–South relations. It is a long-standing concern of the EU, as various existing instruments already demonstrate: European Union–ACP Conventions, regional trade agreements, the General System of Preferences, etc. But as of now all the tools of foreign policy (trade, development, diplomacy), should be devoted to mastering globalization, towards sustainable development, and towards a 'New Deal' for developing countries (the 'coalition for equitable globalization' of Hubert Védrine). The multilateral agenda offers Europe the chance to express itself in the next events following the WTO Doha conference, at the conference on the financing of development (Monterrey, March 2002) and, most importantly, at the Summit on Sustainable Development at Johannesburg, in September 2002, ten years on from the Earth Summit in Rio. The European position should be focused on core issues and structures. We should look to reinforce and make more efficient government aid for development, and the opening of European markets to products from the developing world. As to structures, the Commission should have exclusive competence to negotiate in all major negotiations on international economic governance, as it already does for the Common Trade Policy.

This same logic leads us to envisage the unification of representation in international bodies. This would happen first with the IMF, where it is necessary to move beyond coordination among executive directors, in order to give the euro zone a single representative. The same goes for the World Bank. The process of unification could then be extended to other bodies. It should eventually lead to a unified representation in the UN Security Council.

The Mediterranean world should become the object of a renewed effort on the part of Europeans, without waiting for an enlargement that will displace the geographical priorities of Europe. The Euro-Mediterranean Partnership which began several years ago did not meet its potential. It has not resulted in an intensification of economic links generating development and integration. In the context of 11 September, Europe cannot let this lie fallow. It requires, from 2002, an asymmetrical speeding-up of work towards the Euro-Mediterranean free trade area, which should be accompanied by an increased opening of our agricultural markets; support for public and private investment; and common management of migratory flows.

A new strategic partnership in Europe

The attention given to the governance of globalization and to the South in no way excludes a common project in more directly political and defence fields, or with the East. The new geopolitical situation of Europe, which could potentially bring wider security across the European continent, invites us to develop defence policy, and to give it autonomous means: technological innovation, defence industries, intelligence, etc.

Following on from a European defence identity, Europe should envisage a new strategic partnership with the United States and Russia, which would take account of the reduced substance and legitimacy of NATO, an instrument of the Cold War. This should make all the more sense given that, in the current context, the Americans and Russians seem to be ready to overcome old antagonisms and define new strategic conditions, including on the future of the ABM Treaty. Europe should try to define the conditions for balanced security on the continent, integrating the worries of future Member States – as well as those of Russia – which are careful to preserve the American presence.

We propose:

- *giving the Commission, as in the Common Commercial Policy, the competence to negotiate on all matters relating to the regulation of globalization (environmental negotiations – UN*

environmental conventions on global warming, bio-diversity, bio-security, forests, desertification, organic pollutants etc. – International Maritime Organization, Codex Alimentarius, the dialogue of producers and consumers of petroleum, air transport, commodity organizations, OECD, FATF, WHO, FAO etc.);
- *re-launching the Euro-Mediterranean Partnership;*
- *establishing a unified representation for the euro zone in the IMF, which could then be extended to the World Bank and the UN Security Council;*
- *extending the field of qualified majority voting to questions of human rights for votes at the UN Commission of Human Rights in Geneva;*
- *establishing joint consulates in all major towns.*

Notes

1   We would add here that in the case of the last enlargement, owing to an ideological imbalance in favour of economic and market integration, a tacit agreement was made, which was not in the end respected, based on the idea of keeping the completed *acquis* on the single currency.
2   On this point see the report of the group 'Débat sur l'avenir de l'Europe' chaired by Guy Braibant, La Documentation française, December 2001.
3   Conditional upon the putting in place of a programme of macro-economic convergence, the Cohesion Fund has played a major role in the entry of certain countries into the Euro, by reducing the amount of heavy investment in transport and the environment in national budgets (co-financed at 90%).
4   See the Laeken Declaration on the future of the EU, 15 December 2001, available at www.europa.eu.int.
5   'Nos choix pour l'Europe', *Lettre des Confrontations* (December 2001).
6   Thus, while a majority of the Parliament shared the goals of the Lamfalussy report on speeding up the creation of a European

market for financial services, it did not accept that it should lose its power as co-legislator in order to speed up the adoption of the texts.

7   Article 191 of the Nice Treaty created a legal base for a statute for European political parties on which this would draw.

8   Under this procedure, the Parliament votes on general texts and leaves the executive the means to put them into practice, while still reserving the right to re-examine that practice and to check that it is in line with the meaning of the texts voted upon.

9   The degree of centralization in existing federal organizations is variable.

10 For convenience's sake, we will not distinguish between the ECB, the European System of Central Banks (ESCB) and the Eurosystem.

11 By fixing inflation rates.

12 The ceiling of 2% was broken in June 2000. Inflation is expected to return below that barrier during the first half of 2002.

13 See the Cohen–Mougeot report of the Conseil d'analyse économique. Social policy offers another example of coordination. But a better example is that of defence: the states do not want to lose control of their armed forces, but they look for means of coordinating their use.

14 See the Pisani-Ferry report of the Conseil d'analyse économique on the coordination of economic policies (September 2000), the Communication of the Commission of February 2001, and the Resolution of the European Parliament on the Pervenche Berès report (4 October 2001).

15 With a goal of 67% by January 2005 and 70% before 2010, as against the current figure of 61%.

16 In the same way, the transferability of complementary pensions is not guaranteed.

17 At the edges of this group, and not yet the object of debate in the Council, the development of a supranational system has begun, based on OLAF (a structure of administrative co-operation, generally limited to the defence of the EU's financial interests, but with a considerable potential for expansion).

Conclusion

This essay has worked from two observations: that there is a French malaise on Europe, particularly among the left; and that there are doubts in the European project itself. In both cases, we have formulated a frank diagnosis as to what the future may hold. But our main concern is the risk that these two processes will feed off each other: it is not difficult to imagine how an uncontrolled evolution in the EU could lead to an increased sense of distance from Europe on the part of the French people. Nor is it difficult to work out why disaffection in public opinion could paralyse the country's leaders, lead them to take up defensive positions, and itself prevent them from being a driving force in Europe. In the same way, the absence of France in key debates on Europe's future could contribute to the EU moving in a direction that reinforced its distance from French citizens. The risk that such a vicious circle could develop is real. It is dangerous both for France's role in Europe, and Europe itself.

This risk is of particular concern to the left. Recent history provides examples of the way in which political forces that have played a central role in European integration then become distanced from the process, to a point that they find themselves locked in a position of opposition. Until now this has mainly happened on the right, as seen in the bizarre shift of the British Conservative

Party, which went from securing the UK's entry to progressively sliding into opposition to the euro and to Europe itself. But no political force can pretend to be immune from Euroscepticism, and the left could meet a similar fate if we convince ourselves that European integration is equivalent to liberalization and that the nation state is the only defence against the tyranny of the market. The left might gain some brief intellectual comfort from such a position, but would surely lose both their relevance and influence. The French left would stand idly by as the EU evolved in an opposite direction.

We have argued why we find this way of looking at things mistaken. However, it has the power of simple ideas, can draw on certain facts, and saves us from having to talk to our partners, some of whom would be happy to let France's leaders turn in on themselves, thus isolating their influence to really change things. As a result, although we are convinced that this key moment in Europe's history needs France's contribution more than ever, we need to be ready to consider how, for the first time, European integration could abstain from relying on it.

If this is to be avoided, three conditions need to be met.

Firstly, the French must stop being nostalgic about the old Europe, as if they mourn for the Berlin Wall, and appreciate what has changed in the last fifteen years. Their country will never recover the importance it had when Europe and Germany were divided, but in the eyes of its partners it remains a driving force from which ideas and suggestions are expected.

In order to be influential, France must choose its priorities. It has a lot of determination, but its political and diplomatic capital is not infinite. The energy it expends (and has spent) in defending Franco-German parity, keeping the CAP as it is, or blocking energy market liberalization would undoubtedly have been better devoted to other negotiations, more decisive for the future. Farmers, like workers in the energy industry, would certainly gain more from a proactive attitude than from illusory delaying tactics.

Finally, it is necessary for France's leaders to speak the language of truth about Europe, to say what it has taught us and what we can expect from it. The euro, enlargement, and the discussion on the future of the EU all offer an opportunity. The process will be long, but political impetus cannot wait. The foundations of a new European corner-stone agreement need to be laid already in 2002/3, before the next enlargement. The French left's projects and their vision of the future should be part of this, to their own benefit and that of Europe.